PRAISE FO

Letters to My Friendz

"A very poignant and piercing autobiography, I must say. I think the stories of our lives, no matter how they are told—verbally or written like this, are the best gift we can leave for the next generation. I believe God will send this work to places to comfort and bring hope to generations to come."

Dr. Devine Akhidime
Lecturer, Manchester Metropolitan University, UK

"Writing a book on a topic such as this, with the author sharing her life and personal experiences goes to fulfil the Scriptures where it says, "We loved you so much that we shared with you not only God's Good News but our own lives, too" (1 Thessalonians 2:8). It shows how dear to the heart of the author are the youths of all generations who will read this book. The personal struggles expressed by the author, the temptations and pressures experienced, confirm that in all generations the same temptations are common to young people. The near misses, escapes, and the victories over temptations prove the faithfulness of God, who is available to all generations. Read this book to learn from the wisdom of the wise so you can be wiser."

Michael Oludipe, Pastor in Charge
New Covenant Church Manchester, UK

LETTERS
TO MY
Friendz

ISBN: 978-1-63308-237-3 (paperback)
      978-1-63308-238-0 (ebook)

Interior and Cover Design by R'tor John D. Maghuyop

CHALFANT ECKERT
PUBLISHING

1028 S Bishop Avenue, Dept. 178
Rolla, MO 65401

Printed in United States of America

LETTERS
TO MY
Friendz

Recipe for Building
and Boosting Spiritual Energy

OLIVE ADEBOLA

CHALFANT ECKERT

PUBLISHING

DEDICATION

This book is dedicated to my dear friends
who may be struggling in their journey to know and walk with God.
God has your back, and therefore, you will not fall.

TABLE OF CONTENTS

ACKNOWLEDGEMENTS

I would never have been able to start and complete this project
without the inspiration of the Holy Spirit.

I would like to express my gratitude to my pastors and instructors in
the Lord: Michael and Esther O, Victor Adeyemi, Godwin and Ada I.,
and Dr. Devine A.

Thanks to Rev K.S., Pastor Ayo Jeje, and Sola Olowokere: You were
there from the very beginning of my Christian journey. Becky Elesin,
whose letters encouraged me all through the way, thank you loads.

I owe a debt of gratitude to my beloved daughter, Sophie, and my
friends at NCC Teenage Church for reading this book over and over
again with me. Success, Princess, Esther, and Grace A:
I appreciate you girls!

Many thanks to my editors, Dr. Scott, Greg Baker,
and to Emmanuel Egbetade, Wole Adigun, and Angela Devine for
your helpful suggestions.

Thank you Rev Samson Ajetomobi for inspiring me to write
'Daily Benefits' prayer nugget.

I appreciate my family members at NCC Trafford cell group.
You are the best!

Thanks to Yemi, my friend and prayer partner of over 20 years,
for your encouragement and prayers. I would also like to thank my
many wonderful friends (too numerous to mention) for your immense
support. Tinuke, Bokun, Eki, Seyi, and Bankymoore:
Thanks for being there for me.

A big thanks to my parents and siblings: We are on a journey with
God. Thanks, Bukky A., for your encouragement.

My deepest gratitude to my treasured hubby and amazing children for
your able assistance, guidance, suggestions and loving encouragement
on this task. I am truly blessed and honoured to have you in my life.

FOREWORD

Nothing is more convincing than a personal story, more compelling than tested truth, and more engaging than a transparent life. All of these characterise *Letters to my Friendz*. I wish I had this book or one like it when I was age 13. It would have been my companion through my teenage years. I cannot wait to get it into the hands of my teenage children and indeed every teenager in the world today!

Rev Victor Adeyemi
Founder and Senior Pastor, Global Harvest Int'l Churches
Lagos, Nigeria

PREFACE

Kindness is much like the baton in a relay race. Having received it, it does no good unless you pass it on. Years ago, a girl in a boarding school started choking on some food while eating in the refectory. Although another girl tried to help by slapping her on the back, it was not until one of the kitchen workers rushed over and performed the Heimlich maneuver that the girl's life was saved.

A few years later, a middle-aged woman walking along a dusty road suddenly began having a seizure. A large rock nearby presented a potentially dangerous hazard and only the intervention of a younger woman prevented a potential life-threatening injury. This kind young lady laid the distressed woman flat and gently placed her in the recovery position until the seizure abated. She took care to keep the suffering woman out of harm's way of the dangerous rock and pillowed her head. She then flagged down a car and secured a ride to a nearby hospital where the older woman received treatment. The young lady was the girl who had nearly choked to death years before, and the woman she saved was the very kitchen worker who had saved her.

You have no doubt heard the phrase "One good turn deserves another." I like to put it differently: You are comforted so you can comfort others. Anytime God sends someone your way to comfort or even correct you, this act places you in debt until you return such help to anyone who needs it. Your act of kindness may not be exactly the same as what was done for you, but you should never withhold any act of kindness.

I have questioned volunteers who give freely of their time to help others about why they help, and one answer seems prominent above the others. They are helping because some person or some organization helped them or in some cases their friends or family members. They feel indebted and want to give back what was given to them. Becky was a listening ear for me while I was experiencing different kinds of challenges as a teenager. I believe God allowed me to pass through the challenges I have experienced and brought me out of them so that I could serve as an encouragement to you with the message that *if He can help me through it, He will surely help you through it also.*

I strongly believe the saying that a candle does not lose any of its brightness by lighting another candle. I have written *Letters to My Friendz* with you in mind. I want to use the challenges I experienced as a young teenage Christian to help you through your own struggles as either a young or a new Christian. I am hoping you will be able to take advantage of the practical truths in this book to help you through the challenges every Christian faces in today's world.

Blessed be the God and Father of our Lord Jesus Christ,
the Father of sympathy (pity and mercy) and the God
[Who is the Source] of every comfort (consolation and
encouragement), Who comforts (consoles and encourages) us in
every trouble (calamity and affliction), so that we may also be
able to comfort (console and encourage) those who are in any
kind of trouble or distress, with the comfort (consolation and
encouragement) with which we ourselves are comforted
(consoled and encouraged) by God.

2 Corinthians 1:3-4 (AMP)

I bear the scars from having been through many of the issues and pains you are facing, and I hope the wisdom I have gleaned will comfort as well as challenge you to persevere towards maturity.

Warmly yours

CHAPTER 1

MY STRUGGLES

Dear Friend,

Christian adults are sometimes quick to point accusing fingers at young people who make poor choices or fail to live up to the adult's idea of Christianity. It sometimes seems as though we live in a completely different world. I must admit that I used to be one of those grown-ups. I would see moral failure among some Christians and conclude that they were not genuinely saved. "No sincere Christian would do that," I would quip.

I found this judgmental attitude easy until a few years back when I recalled my own teenage years and the struggles I went through and the help God sent my way. I now appreciate the challenges young people have to deal with while living in an ungodly environment. I wish to seize this opportunity to commend teenagers and young adults for the courage they demonstrate in expressing themselves in matters relating to sex, peer pressure, self-identity, low self-esteem, depression, and even suicide. Unlike us (grown-ups), they are more open to explore – even to explore the possibilities of new directions should their choices prove traumatic.

SHOULD I WALK YOU THROUGH?

Whether you call it *swag* or the latest fad, it is easy to tell what's important to most young people today. Sagging jeans, piercings and tattoos, selfies on Instagram, countless likes on Facebook, Smartphone messaging, secret sexting during sleepovers ... you get my drift? Here's the deal: I understand! I remember growing up with similar desires. I wanted to be noticed by the boys, too. I wondered what it would be like to go partying with friends. I even wondered what my first kiss would be like and so much more, but this was not how my story began.

I was born into a Christian family and had always been faithful in attending church. I attended a white-garment church with my parents, so I had an idea of who God was and what He expected of me. I grew up reading the Bible, especially the book of Psalms, and praying. Though I found the church service tedious, repetitive, and boring, I was spurred by the blaring hymns, carefree dance, and impassioned prayers. I remember participating fully in church activities. I sang in the choir and attended Bible studies, but my inner yearning for God was never satisfied.

Years later, my eldest sister came home from boarding school claiming to have had a spiritual transformation. "I have been born again," she told us. She went on to tell the family stories of Hell and Heaven and said we could escape Hell by renouncing our sins and accepting Jesus' forgiveness by faith. "The moment you do that," she said ecstatically, "you likewise would be born again."

Without a moment's hesitation, my other sisters and I repeated some prayers led by my oldest sister. To be honest, I didn't feel any different. I had heard how others experienced a feeling of peace the moment they said *The Sinner's Prayer*. Not me. What did change, however, was what happened during my private time with God. God had moved from the confines of white garments and tasteless rhetoric into my priceless heart. Christianity was no longer a religion to me; it became real, practical, and personal. I could enjoy intimacy with God and the assurance of His abiding presence with me.

My life continued to change. I found that a lot of popular music and literature contradicted my understanding of what it meant to love God and people, and as a result I trashed the few collections I had and replaced them with songs and literature that reflected my spiritual awakening. What's more, as I grew fonder of God, I began to love people more deeply. I did, however, see the wisdom in choosing close friends who shared my spiritual experience. Getting involved in an intimate relationship soon lost its appeal, and my dad, who was once hesitant about the faith, began to notice the transformation in his daughters. For instance, we would stay indoors and share our sincere love for God in singing/worshiping and participating in a weekly fast. My dad began to ask us to pray for him whenever he took ill or his business took a downturn.

Our love for God and others inspired us to sacrifice various self-serving conveniences. Even though we became members of a Pentecostal church, I found it a sharp contrast to what I was accustomed to. Not only was it a different system of worship compared to my former church but the teachings were stringent and largely unforgiving. It seemed that every mistake, no matter how seemingly minor, was met with disapproval and severe judgment. Therefore, I concealed my struggles as best as I could and made sure I dressed modestly and looked the part – pious.

Not long after I began my secondary education at the age of eleven, I met a group of older students who were also born again. I attended a Roman Catholic boarding school and lived on campus, so the girls there became my friends. These older students truly encouraged me in my new faith, and I was fortunate to have met them. At the same time, I also found acceptance with a group of unbelieving students. Being included in this latter group had an advantage – it reduced the amount of bullying I experienced. But, these girls were lesbians who partied a lot and were known to cheat on exams.

I was constantly exposed to filthy thinking and immorality. One of the girls asked if I had ever kissed or had sex with a girl before and volunteered to teach me. I was only eleven years old! She would sneak into my room and worm her way under the mosquito net and blankets to teach me how to kiss.

I dared not report this to the teachers or other students. No one would believe me because these girls had managed to gain the faculty's trust. I did tell the few Christian girls there, but they couldn't protect me much. Eventually, I had to learn to stand up for myself. Unless you have been in a situation like this, you cannot imagine the abuse that takes place in boarding schools. Neither the teachers nor the headmasters nor even the police could protect you. At that time, social workers and child protective services did not even exist!

My young Christian life became full of condemnation, guilt, mental struggles, insecurity, low self-esteem, anger, and unforgiveness. I grew worried about so many things that I could not focus on my academics and performed below expectations. I worried mainly about falling below God's expectations and ending up in Hell.

As if that was not enough, I was not exempt from feeling inadequate. I could not recall exactly how and why I wallowed in low self-esteem, but I was very hard on myself. My grades were not good enough, and I would compare myself with others who were doing well. I could not seem to discover anything I was good at. I would occasionally be happy when I performed well in a subject, but whenever I failed I would think of ending my life.

The devil tormented my mind so much that I could not see anything good about my existence. I was born into a polygamous family and therefore suffered so much guilt and helplessness because I could not change or correct the circumstance surrounding my birth. I was quite unsettled and definitely not a happy child. I struggled to assimilate when I studied and spent hours in the classroom with little to show for it.

I recall a particular day after failing in Fine Art class. I was so distraught I decided to end my life by downing a cocktail of cleaning products. My life was spared only by God's divine grace. The schoolteachers definitely made things worse for me. I was called names such as "pretty for nothing," "lazy bones," "sickly," and so on. It became completely impossible to open up to any teacher or counselor.

Who could help? Who would believe and intervene for this helpless teenager?

Warmly yours

CHAPTER 2

TIMELY HELP

Dear Friend,

Growing up as a Christian teenager was not easy for me. It had its challenges and difficulties, but God was kind to me and sent people my way who helped me through those turbulent years. One such person was Becky, a medical student at a distant university who wrote me letters that became a light in an otherwise dark time of my life. She was an exemplary young Christian adult who came into my life during a time when I was struggling mentally with many things.

I was seriously considering suicide, thinking it might be my only way out. Though I had hoped that becoming born again would transform my mind instantly, it simply did not work that way for me. My mind was still as polluted and grubby as ever. I would respond to altar calls and pray with the preachers or other students –after all, the Bible says that if I took such steps of faith that old things would pass away and all things would become new. But the inner struggles in my heart and mind remained. I was ashamed of what was going on inside of me and never brought it up with anyone ... but God knew. He knew my struggles with anger, rejection, unforgiveness, hatred, fear of failure, and suicidal and immoral thoughts.

That is where my dear friend Becky's letters made a difference. They became a lifeline that I clung to desperately. They encouraged me to continue in the Word of God, to keep praying, and to be strong in the faith, which was a real challenge in the dark boarding school atmosphere. Every time I got one of her letters, it would make my entire day. From the moment I saw Becky's letter, I would not be able to stop smiling. I couldn't wait to read her words and share them with my friends. Her letters relieved much stress in my life.

I recall one very hot day in the boarding school. Since it was a Roman Catholic school, we were required to have devotions in which we recited the *Angelus* (the Angelus is a Roman Catholic devotion that commemorates the Incarnation of Jesus and includes saying the *Hail Mary* at morning, noon, and sunset). I was looking forward to the end of the prayers when mail would be passed out. With all the excitement bubbling up inside me, it was difficult to concentrate on the prayers or the national and school anthems.

Four weeks had passed since Becky's last letter had come, and someone had mentioned that I had mail that day. I just knew it was from her. Sure enough, my name was called and I was handed a letter from Becky! Just knowing she had written to me was such a boost to my spirit. It helped me realize that God had never been surprised or shocked at my mistakes, that He still loved me. We cannot jolt God – no matter what we do. He knows our sinful condition, and He has already made provision for our weaknesses. Do not misunderstand me. God is never happy when we sin. He is disappointed when we sin, but He knows our frame. He sees the end from the beginning, and He extends grace and mercy towards us.

I carefully observed Becky's way of life, which matched what she wrote in her letters to me. She encouraged me to develop a close relationship with God and a wholesome thought life through reflecting on the Bible. I received a lot of assurance that God was not judging me and that I could live right if I desired to and return to Him if I wandered off. I will share with you in this book some biblical truths that Becky shared with me in her letters and during our discussions as well as the lessons I learnt by studying the way she lived out the Bible.

The remarkable route of my escape from some of my struggles was understanding and declaring my redemption. Initially, I found the steps to salvation too easy to accept as true. How could a person simply declare his or her faith through a prayer and expect to go to Heaven or become a righteous child of God? I struggled with the simplicity of it. In fact, I believe I am not alone in that. Many have a similar struggle, thinking there has to be more to it, more they must do or become to attain redemption. But here is the truth: *It is that simple!* We are not asked to do spiritual gymnastics, engage in soul travel, become martyrs of the faith, or pay an exorbitant amount of money, salvation is a free gift of God for all who accept it.

Acts 16:31 provides a simple answer to the question about how we are saved. Yes, salvation is as simple as believing and confessing the Lordship of Jesus Christ and accepting His forgiveness of your sins. It is so easy because what Jesus did was so hard. Jesus paid a great price with His own shed blood for our sins. Without the shedding of blood, there is no forgiveness of sin. To receive this forgiveness is to be saved, and to be saved we must only take the personal responsibility to confess Christ. The conviction of your heart is what brings you to confess Him. Have you accepted the forgiveness that Jesus offers? If not, while you still have time, discover that Jesus Christ is worthy of being your life's guide. He gave His life for you, and all you have to do is believe that He died on the Cross, was buried, and then rose again from the dead.

If you acknowledge and confess with your lips that Jesus is Lord
and in your heart believe (adhere to, trust in, and rely on the truth)
that God raised Him from the dead, you will be saved.

Romans 10:9 (AMP)

Yes! It's that simple. Simply ask Him to forgive your sins and save you. Millions have already made this wise choice, and I promise you that you will never regret giving your life to Him—since He gave His life to keep yours from Hell!

You cannot save yourself, and you cannot work your way into Heaven. I tried my best to do all the right things, but I couldn't do it alone. I attended fellowship and church meetings and repented whenever I sinned, but I continued to struggle. I wanted to serve God with vitality, but I couldn't see past by own trials. I made many New Year's resolutions only to break them repeatedly. It was maddening. I wanted to live a holy life but felt as though I couldn't, that I was doomed to live in misery and sin all my days. Has this been your experience, too? If so, know that the Apostle Paul understood our feelings and struggles because he also struggled. In Romans 7:14 (CEB), he wrote:

> *I know that all God's commands are spiritual, but I'm not.*
> *Isn't this also your experience? Yes. I'm full of myself—after all,*
> *I've spent a long time in sin's prison. What I don't understand about*
> *myself is that I decide one way, but then I act another, doing things*
> *I absolutely despise. For if I know the law but still can't keep it, and*
> *if the power of sin within me keeps sabotaging my best intentions,*
> *I obviously need help! I realize that I don't have what it takes.*
> *I can will it, but I can't do it. I decide to do well, but I don't really*
> *do it; I decide not to do bad, but then I do it anyway … I've tried*
> *everything and nothing helps. I'm at the end of my rope.*
> *s there no one who can do anything for me?*

This is an incredible confession from one of the great men of faith in the Bible. Paul was a Christian when he wrote this. It shows how being a Christian does not necessarily mean that we will not struggle. You, like me and all the rest of us, probably find that you fall well short of God's standard. You may wonder if it is even possible to please God—His expectations are very high! You may have asked for forgiveness many times for the same thing. Trying hard in your own power will not enable you to live above sin. Paul wrote in Romans 7:25 (CEB):

Thank God through Jesus Christ our Lord!
Jesus acted to set things right in this life of contradictions where
I want to serve God with all my heart and mind, but I am pulled
by the influence of sin to do something totally different.

What all young Christians (teenagers/young adults) and new (or old) converts need to do is this: Accept on faith that what Jesus did on the Cross was your victory over sin! You must understand that Jesus not only died to forgive your sins but to give you the grace to triumph over them. The power of the flesh (sin) can be overwhelming, but the Spirit of God can curtail the flesh. The key to defeating the flesh is to strengthen the Spirit within you. You need to be aware of what can drain your spiritual strength and what you can do to boost your spiritual energy.

Dear Friend, one additional thing you can do is to seek help the moment you need it. Trying to hide your weaknesses and struggles is a recipe for disaster. I find it disappointing that some young people refuse to ask for help. Young people in this day and age try to be self-sufficient and independent. Though an independent attitude can be good in many arenas, it can also be dangerous when it comes to your walk with God. You need people who can support you and help you to grow—just like Becky did for me.

Asking for help is essential to overcoming many of the things in your life that seek to drain away your inner strength. You won't go wrong if you ask help of the right people. There is safety in the multitude of counsellors. Do not walk alone!

Warmly Yours

CHAPTER 3

WHO AM I?

Dear Friend,

An English teacher in a grammar school used to counsel her students against getting involved in sexual relationships as teenagers. She would say, "Don't eat your soup while it is boiling hot because if you do, you will scald your tongue and not enjoy the rest of the soup." Though her students would laugh at this statement, some of them took her seriously and decided not to go into any sexual relationships. One student, however, was in a hurry as some young people are. She had looked forward to having her first kiss and experiencing a sexual relationship. Unfortunately, she became pregnant at an early age of fourteen. She was afraid to confide in her parents about it, so she kept her pregnancy a top secret.

At some point during her pregnancy, she stopped attending school because she couldn't cope with school work due to severe morning sickness. Soon after, she began to have pain in her abdomen. Thinking it was just a symptom of early pregnancy, she did not disclose it to her parents. When her condition grew worse, her parents thought she had typhoid fever and treated her for this ailment.

The pain increased until it became unbearable. The poor girl decided to self-medicate because she feared that further investigation would reveal that she was pregnant. Little did she know that she had an ectopic pregnancy. She was eventually taken to the hospital for treatment, where the truth was revealed. When she was asked if she knew she was pregnant, she denied it with her last breath. As she was being wheeled into the theatre room for emergency surgery, she gave up the ghost. A future, a star, a glorious tomorrow died that day on the platform of a secret sin of sex! This distressing incident led me to vow not to indulge in premarital sex.

Starting an intimate relationship as a teenager may stem from the quest for affirmation. The poor girl above was one who needed someone to affirm her. She did not have a healthy relationship with her parents. She needed someone to love and tell her she could achieve things in life. She had no real sense of her worth, and people around her had a low opinion of her abilities.

Growing up comes with a load of questions: Who am I? What is my purpose in life? What is my mission and my identity as a person? Defining one's identity and coming to terms with the realities of life can be challenging, but you will do yourself a lot of good if you do not compare yourself to others. Life may seem to go smoothly for some people; some seem to have it all rosy and their lives seem enviable and full of supposedly treasured moments. The truth is: God has a good plan for you, too.

We all have challenges and opportunities, and we all have strengths and weaknesses. The sayings "not all that glitters is gold" and "the grass is not necessarily greener on the other side" are very apt. We all have opportunities and challenges. The key is knowing how to stay positive and focused on God when we are going through challenges.

To discover your identity is to realise that you are unique: body and soul; you are marvelously made! God created you for definite purposes and hence gave you a distinct DNA. Even identical twins have identifiable mutations in their DNA at the mitochondrial level. This reinforces the fact that you are created and designed for specific purposes in life. It is proof that you do not have to compare your life with others because you are unique. Make peace with yourself at all times and smile always. Do not expect others to understand your journey if they have never walked your path. Walk straight and be focused and determined to be who God wants you to be. You can regain your self-worth when you realise that you are different from others: You are unique, distinct, have your own path to chart, and have your own story to tell. Look at yourself in the mirror and love what you see. What you see is perfect for God's purpose! When you get to that state of mind and accept and internalise it, you will surely find peace and happiness with yourself, your Creator, and your world, and it will be visible to others. You do not need anyone to validate yourself. You are simply wonderful!

A sexual relationship as a teenager and outside marriage is a distraction. It will not give you the love and joy that you need. Only God loves unconditionally. Therefore, as 1 Peter 2:9 guides, you should starve your distractions, nurture your focus, and maintain your identity.

Warmly Yours

CHAPTER 4

A SUPERMAN

Dear Friend,

We all make decisions to do the right thing sometimes but then lack the strength and the staying power to follow through. Being resolute about your decision might require encouragement from people who have been through the same situation. As we will see, great physical power was not enough to ward off sexual temptation for a guy like Samson.

Most of us are familiar with the word *strength*, which the Oxford English Dictionary defines as "the quality or the state of being physically strong." But strength also means the power to resist attack and the ability to maintain a strong moral or intellectual position.

The glory of the young is their strength

Proverbs 20:29

Young men typically take great pride and pleasure in their physical strength, but to have spiritual strength is to be able to resist the wiles and tricks of the devil. Spiritual strength enables one to withstand peer pressure and to avoid becoming a victim. I pray you will never lose your spiritual strength!

Young people revel in their vitality and strength, but how miserable are those who are young but frail? Strength allows for vigorous resistance when we come under attack. When we are strong, we are confident, determined, and ready. In this modern age, however, too many things seek to sap our strength and thus rob us of our magnificence, splendour, grandeur, majesty, and greatness! Such strength drainers come in many guises such as the media, ungodly government policies, and worldly philosophies. These things are subtle, and often we find ourselves drawn into them without any resistance at all. Although it is a difficult task to maintain spiritual strength, with God, everything is possible!

Strength is more than just physical. Young people are fascinated with a person's looks and physical prowess. We become obsessed with losing weight, working out, becoming muscular and getting into shape, looking pretty, and so on. Some invest a lot of time in acquiring new skills or more knowledge, thinking education will be the answer to their problems and will secure their futures. Though none of that is inherently bad, we should develop the same obsession for becoming spiritually strong in the Lord. We need to build our spiritual muscles so that we can effectively resist the evil we encounter on a daily basis. Physical strength will not stop the fiery darts of the wicked one, which are spiritual.

Samson, the strongest man who ever lived, was brought low by a much "weaker" woman. Today, we would consider him to be akin to Superman or the Incredible Hulk—a giant among men, someone capable of defeating entire armies single-handedly. Perhaps we can learn something from this superman's life. Let's consider Judges 13 (AMP):

> *And the Angel of the Lord appeared to the woman and said to her,*
> *Behold, you are barren and have no children, but you shall become*
> *pregnant and bear a son. Therefore beware and drink no wine or*
> *strong drink and eat nothing unclean … And Manoah said,*
> *now when your words come true, how shall we manage the child,*
> *and what is he to do? And the Angel of the Lord said to Manoah,*

Let the mother beware of all that I told her. And the woman [in due time] bore a son and called his name Samson; and the child grew and the Lord blessed him.

The Scripture above tells the story of the amazing birth of Samson. The Lord used Samson mightily, enabling him to accomplish unusual things that we would consider superhuman. His father, however, understood that such a miraculous child would need to be raised uniquely, so he asked God for guidance, which is important. If children and young people are not supervised and directed, they run a greater risk of making serious mistakes. Manoah wanted to know how to raise and supervise Samson appropriately.

In civilised societies, it is a criminal offense to leave a child unsupervised. Yet, once a person is born again into the family of God, where are those who should be supervising and guiding these infant Christians? Young Christians may make serious spiritual mistakes unless they are guided into the truth of the Word of God. It is spiritually criminal on the part of more mature believers to leave these new Christians at the mercy of a wicked and unmerciful world. Because young Christians are often left alone, it is no surprise that some stray.

Despite Samson's parents' attempts to guide him, Samson chose to disobey. You also have a choice. God will not force you to serve Him against your will. Samson took a Philistine wife in opposition to his parents' wishes. He left his new wife in a fury when she betrayed him, revealing the answer to a riddle and spoiling his bet with some of the young men at his wedding feast. He killed thirty men to make good on his bet. Eventually, he returned to his wife only to find out that she had been given to another man – his best friend.

So Samson went and caught three hundred foxes; and took torches, and turning the foxes tail to tail, and put a torch between each pair of tails. When he had set the torches on ablaze, he let the foxes go

into the standing grain of the Philistines, and burned up the shocks
and the standing grain, along with the olive orchards....

Judges 15:4-5, 8 (AMP)

This man had no self-control! Naturally, his rampage angered the Philistines who demanded that Samson be turned over to them. Fearful of their wrath, 3,000 men of Samson's own people from Judah went and arrested Samson to take him to the Philistines. They tied him up with two new ropes and brought him to the Philistine army.

"We promise," the men said. "We will only tie you up and turn
you over to the Philistines. We won't kill you." Then they tied up
his hands and arms with two brand-new ropes and led him away
from Etam Rock. When the Philistines saw that Samson was being
brought to their camp at Jawbone, they started shouting and ran
toward him. But the Lord's Spirit took control of Samson, and
Samson broke the ropes, as though they were pieces of burnt cloth.

Judges 15:14-15

Whoa! A Superman indeed! With superhuman strength from God, Samson was certainly an Old Testament "Superman." He seemed invincible, but a short while after this, his strength left him when he betrayed the last of his vows and indulged in immorality, disobedience, and anger. One day while Samson was in Gaza, he saw a prostitute and went to her house to spend the night (Judges 16:1-4). It's a shame that because of sexual immorality, Samson gave up the secret to his great strength and found himself powerless, betrayed by the woman with whom he had fallen in love. God's thoughts about immorality are clear.

Don't you know that those doing such things have no share in the
Kingdom of God? Don't fool yourselves. Those who live immoral
lives, who are idol worshipers, adulterers or homosexuals—will
have no share in his Kingdom. Neither will thieves or greedy people,

drunkards, slanderers, or robbers. There was a time when some of you were just like that but now your sins are washed away, and you are set apart for God; and he has accepted you because of what the Lord Jesus Christ and the Spirit of our God have done for you.

1 Corinthians 6:9-11 (CEB)

Samson's story is one of a downward spiral. He went from bad to worse until at last he was weak and blind and a laughingstock. The woman he loved, Delilah, turned on him for money, just as Judas turned on Jesus for thirty pieces of silver.

Dear Friend, Delilah's greed overwhelmed any feelings she might have had for Samson. She wanted that money and nagged Samson until he gave in and told her the secret of his strength. She used his love for her against him to entice him to reveal his secret. Samson isn't alone. There are people around us who try to entice us and steal our spiritual strength. We've all been enticed, and at some point I dare say chances are good that we have all fallen prey to it. Sin always looks attractive, and it is always enticing.

I will share with you the wise words of Solomon in Proverbs 1:10 (ESV). Solomon knew we could be enticed at some point by the pleasures of the world (he knew this from experience), so he gave this warning: "If sinners entice you, please do not consent." One thing is sure: You will definitely be enticed, but you should know how to respond. Your reaction can only be firm if you have enough inner strength to resist the temptation.

As for Samson, if you are unfamiliar with the rest of the story, you should read it. It took time, but eventually Samson capitulated and told Delilah wherein his strength lay. She pressed him day after day, using tears and his love for her against him, until he felt so vexed he just gave in to shut her up. Delilah cut his hair while he lay sleeping and then turned him over to the Philistine lords (Judges 16:16-19). Samson's hair was part of his Nazarite vow to God. If it was cut, the last part of his vow and pledge to God would be cut. In the blindness of his own immorality, he did not see Delilah's deception until it was too late.

We can learn many lessons from the life of Samson, but one thing is certain. The devil knows your weaknesses. He knows your habits, including the immoral ones, which puts him in a position to use your weaknesses against you. He knows that some things may be more appealing to you than others. Remember, however, that the devil is not all-knowing. He cannot discern your thoughts. David wrote in Psalm 139:1:

> *O Lord, you have searched me and known me!*
> *You know when I sit down and when I rise up;*
> *you discern my thoughts from afar.*
> *You search out my path and my lying down*
> *and are acquainted with all my ways.*

Thank God that the devil does not know all these things about you. Only God can search and discern your thoughts.

Although the devil may know your weaknesses and seek to destroy you, God also knows your weaknesses and seeks to strengthen you when you make a decision to dwell with Him. Having mentioned that, I can say confidently that God is always good and the devil is ever bad. God sent His Son to give you eternal life, but the devil is a murderer, a thief, and a destroyer! He hates God and thinks he can hurt God by hurting you. He wants to drain you of your spiritual strength and render you too weak to resist his attacks. You must recognise your own weaknesses and fortify yourself against the ever-present danger that the devil wants to use those weaknesses against you.

The final chapter of Samson's life brought tears to my eyes. I wonder how sad God becomes when He sees His children fall prey to the cheap tricks of the enemy, especially after God has forewarned them of those tricks. It is strange how most toddlers will keep their distance from a hot stove or a fireplace because their parents have warned them about it. We have been warned, too, but all too often we still get burned by sin. If we had the faith of a child to just trust God, we would be able to escape much evil in our lives. Consider what happened to Samson:

> *"But the Philistines laid hold of him, bored out his eyes, and*
> *brought him down to Gaza and bound him with [two] bronze*
> *fetters; and he ground at the mill in the prison. But the hair of his*
> *head began to grow again after it had been shaved. Then Samson*
> *called to the Lord and said, O Lord God, [earnestly] remember me,*
> *I pray You, and strengthen me, I pray You, only this once, O God,*
> *and let me have one vengeance upon the Philistines for both my*
> *eyes. And Samson laid hold of the two middle pillars by which the*
> *house was borne up, one with his right hand and the other with*
> *his left. And Samson cried, let me die with the Philistines! And he*
> *bowed himself mightily, and the house fell upon the princes and*
> *upon all the people that were in it. So the dead whom he slew at his*
> *death were more than they whom he slew in his life.*

Judges 16 (AMP)

Without a sliver of doubt, physical strength is not sufficient to keep us from falling prey to immorality, addiction, bad habits, and other besetting sins. You cannot do it on your own. You would think Samson, with his great strength, could have resisted sin's temptation. But although he was physically strong, he was spiritually weak. In the chapters that follow, we will learn how we can build our spiritual strength to escape being devoured by the enemy (the devil) and enjoy a good and stable relationship with God.

Finally, Dear Friend, before you read on, I would like to tell you that there is a miracle in your mouth. You can have whatever you say. If you believe, make these confessions by faith, and God will respond to your requests.

Warmly Yours

CHAPTER 5

STRENGTH DRAINER

Dear Friend,

I was shocked to find out just how far our society had descended when I heard on the news that prostitution was no longer illegal. Selling your body – or even someone else's – for sex has come to be seen as perfectly acceptable. What has happened to our society? Do we call this civilisation?

Dear Friend, we should not dismiss the lessons of Samson, who sold his strength because of sexual immorality and died lonely, surrounded by his enemies. What are we as a society doing when we sell our spiritual strength for the pleasures of immorality? What will become of our young people? We are weakened as a society because we have believed the lies the devil has told us.

Our youth are under fierce attack. They are being systematically destroyed and becoming morally weak. The only way to prevent this is to identify those things that drain us of our spiritual strength. Perhaps the most obvious one is sexual immorality. By this, I mean fornication, which is sex before or outside of marriage. The New Testament Greek word *porneia* is often translated in English as fornication. It is also the root of the word pornography. Lust, which is frequently misunderstood as love, is considering impure sexual desires in the mind. Homosexuality is sex between people of the same gender, and masturbation, which is self-sex, is also on the rise.

Some young people argue that masturbation is okay since one is not having penetrative sex with anyone else. Masturbation, however, is a form of sexual self-gratification, not something that God intended sex to be. God intended sex to be a mutually pleasing experience between a husband and a wife, a part of a much greater holy relationship. It was never meant to be something to gratify oneself. Although the Bible doesn't mention masturbation in particular, the Scriptures do have a lot to say about the proper use of God's gift of sex. It is meant to be the consummation of the relationship between a husband and a wife. Anything outside of that is not acceptable to God.

I read in an article in *What About Jesus?* that some doctors recommend masturbation as a form of therapeutic exercise to alleviate overwhelming sexual desire. According to them, masturbation is a way to wean a person away from more serious sexual malfunction. They see it, however, as a purely biological function, not as a spiritual act ordained by God for a husband and wife. Committing the "lesser" sin of masturbation to avoid a so-called "greater" sexual sin does not justify the act.

The world obviously knows that sex sells. In advertising, the association of sexual images with a particular product or service is a well-known tactic to generate revenue. That is why some ads feature sexy, half-naked females and handsome young (often shirtless) men. The actors and models are always happy and excited and sexual arousal is a major part of the advertising theme. They never show a drunken man lying in his own vomit on a park bench. Sex is attractive to us and the world obviously uses it to draw us in on numerous levels.

Our society encourages young people to become sexually active at young ages. They provide "safe sex" items such as condoms and birth control pills. So instead of teaching young people self-control, society encourages young people to "rut" like animals. Indeed, they view young people as nothing more than animals in this regard. It is disgusting and completely against what the Word of God teaches.

Sexual immorality breeds many social ills and corrupts a person's thinking about a lot of things. Those who vow to abstain and maintain a moral walk are mocked and ridiculed. In some communities, teenage boys measure "manhood" by the number of girls they have had sex with. Even girls, to some degree, measure their womanhood by how young they were when they lost their virginity. God is certainly not pleased with these measurements.

Several young people have asked me, "If sexual feelings are bad, why did God create them and why can't I have sex?" Well, of course, you can have sex in the appropriate relationship and at the right time – in marriage. True, God created us with sexual desires, which which are good and holy feelings. Unfortunately, the purpose of sex has changed over the years from a physical and spiritual union of husband and wife to the fulfillment of indiscriminate and uncontrolled lustful desires. Please understand that to reach your goals in life, you must have self-control and set boundaries in your relationships with members of the opposite sex.

Setting boundaries is proof of self-respect, and is an essential part of the ground rules when starting a relationship. It is good to learn how to discipline your body, thoughts, and feelings at a young age because you cannot live a godly life without self-control or discipline. Think about the consequences of every action you take that includes premarital sex. I do not know of any negative consequence of abstaining from premarital sex, but I do know loads of deadly consequences of indulging in it.

The Bible teaches us that there is a time for everything. The time and place for sex is in marriage. Learning to delay gratification is an essential part of growing unto maturity! This may seem like an old-fashioned belief, but the Word of God applies to every generation in every age. Never forget that God has your best interests at heart, and so His commandments can only benefit you. Do not be fooled into the perverted thinking that sex outside of marriage is okay. It is not – and nothing good will come of it.

Warmly Yours

CHAPTER 6

FLEE IF IT LOOKS LIKE EVIL

Dear Friend,

A pretty Christian girl – we'll call her Laura – started a friendship with a good-looking and seemingly decent guy who had no real commitment to his Christian faith. In college, they became reading mates, but their relationship quickly progressed to a "special friendship." They enjoyed each other's company so much that they spent time alone in her room till it was very late in the night. Although she occasionally worried about having him alone in her room at such ungodly hours, Laura quietly ignored the red flags. Over time, the guy began to touch her inappropriately during study time, and a few friends even expressed concerns about the inappropriateness of the physical contact. Laura dismissed their concerns with a wave of her hand and told them not to worry.

Having thrown all inhibition overboard, they started having secret rendezvous. The relationship quickly grew intimate, and they began to kiss and have sex on a regular basis. Although Laura was not completely happy after any of these experiences, the guy told her that God was not going to kill them for having sex. This turn of events began to take a toll on her commitment to her faith. She often avoided Christian friends and activities. This continued for a while and she even aborted a few pregnancies. While Laura kept all these activities secret, the guy bragged to his friends about his conquest.

After a few abortions, Laura opened up to a young Christian friend who was completely in shock to learn of Laura's abortions. She counseled Laura, however, to stand up for herself if she wanted to end the relationship and encouraged her to speak to a more mature person. When Laura told the guy that she had opened up to a friend, he scolded her and reinforced that she should never speak to anyone about their special relationship.

Unfortunately, Laura listened to the guy's "sweet nothings" as he promised they would get engaged. So a short time later, he proposed marriage and they became engaged. Everything seemed perfect until a few months later when the guy told Laura that he preferred a more decent girl to marry and dumped her. Laura was completely devastated and did not get over this regrettable incident.

Dear Friend, sexual immorality thrives in darkness. When the Word of God resides in your heart, however, immorality is brought into the light so you can see it for what it is. The Bible says that the Word of the Lord brings light. Darkness is merely the absence of light. The only way darkness can linger is if you turn off the light. The heart of man is naturally evil, unclean, and filthy, but when you allow the Word of God into your heart, this evil is illuminated and cleansed.

The entrance of your words gives light; their unfolding gives understanding (discernment and comprehension) to the simple

Psalm 119:130 (AMP)

Hence, if you are willing to accept God's Word, light will shine into the darkness of your heart. The secret to living a holy life is to fill your heart with an adequate amount of the Word of God so you will not act on what the devil suggests to you. Do everything in your power to retain the Word in your heart!

I keep your word close, in my heart, so that I won't sin against you.

Psalm 119:11 (CEB)

Be Alert!

Be aware of what you watch and what you listen to. Enough distractions exist just going out into the world that you don't need to invite them into your house or go out of your way to watch them. Above all, be careful what you think because your thoughts control your life (Proverbs 4:23 CEB).

I am aware that television and the Internet have become a part of our daily lives. They have a huge influence on how we think and act. Young people in particular spend a lot of time in front of the screen, and there is no doubt that they are influenced by the messages they receive. Although I do not think that all television programs are bad and there are certainly good uses of the Internet, unless we are careful we will expose ourselves to worldly philosophies that will begin to impact our thinking.

Television and the Internet may influence our understanding of beauty, love, sex, and even what clothes to buy! We come to believe that we must look a certain way to be pretty or handsome and have certain type of lovers in our lives. Media teaches us that sexual immorality is a good thing and brings no harm. The more we watch it, the more it influences our thinking and our beliefs.

NAKED AND BLIND

When I was a teenager, I deceived myself into believing that the music I listened to and the books I read had no influence on my life. I was not being honest. Those things did influence me. When I hear of a murder or a terrorist act, I cannot help but wonder sadly what was going on in the perpetrator's mind. Who or what influenced him? When did he stop being honest with himself and give in wholeheartedly to the darkness—somehow believing it was light?

Music is a powerful tool. In God's hands, it brings majesty and honour to Him. In the devil's hands, it uplifts the flesh and puts us on a path of destruction. Songs and their lyrics stick with us and we can recall them years later. Be wise in choosing the music you listen to. What does the music you listen to uplift and promote? Sex, sin, or self? Or does it honour God? I'm not advocating that songs must always have gospel lyrics, but they must promote the values you espouse and not encourage anything violent or immoral.

David, the most renowned musician in the Bible, used music for worship. In fact, when King Saul was troubled by an evil spirit, it was David's hand on the harp that eased Saul's suffering and brought restoration to his troubled soul (1 Samuel 16:14-23). Music is indeed a potent, inspiring, and therapeutic resource if used appropriately.

In the New Testament, the Apostle Paul teaches Christians to encourage one another with music (Ephesians 5:19). You should consider the lyrics when choosing music. Although it is not specifically speaking of music, Philippians 4:8 (AMP) is a great guide to the kinds of lyrics that honor God and bring wholesome enjoyment.

> *For the rest, brethren, whatever is true, whatever is worthy of reverence and is honourable and decent, whatever is just, whatever is pure, whatever is lovely and lovable, whatever is kind and winsome and gracious, if there is any virtue and excellence, if there is anything worthy of praise, think on and weigh and take account of these things [fix your minds on them].*

Secular music to a large degree does not meet the standard of Philippians 4:8. Do the songs you listen to uphold godly values? Keep in mind that whatever you allow to occupy your mind will eventually come out in your words and actions.

Be honest about what you watch, listen to, and read. Look at it through the lens of the Word of God. It is much easier to keep holy vows when you are reinforcing those vows with what you listen to and what you watch. It is much harder to keep those vows when you are constantly filling your mind with things that seek to tempt you to break those vows. Remember, garbage in, garbage out. Godliness in, godliness out.

If you have been involved in sex outside of marriage or anything immoral based on peer pressure or what you have watched and listened to, know that God is a merciful God who is ready to forgive. He will not condemn you, and neither will I. Remember that today is the first day of the rest of your life. You have this day to start out fresh and make the rest of your life holy and incredible for God. Jesus will forgive you and wash you clean if you ask Him. Will you?

Warmly Yours

Notes

- How honest are you about what you listen to and what you read?
- Are there books you read that do not add value to your life and morals?
- What are you listening to that stimulates sinful passions?
- How do you plan to guard against ungodliness?

CHAPTER 7

"And Lead Us Not Into Temptation"

Dear Friend,

The Lord's Prayer was one of the most often-said prayers when I was a teenager, but do people really understand that prayer? Do you understand that when you ask God to keep you from temptation that you also have a part to play? There were a few strict rules while I was in courtship. You could not visit your fiancé without a chaperon, let alone sleep over at his house. This simple rule didn't make much sense to me until years later. My pastor, family, and friends were only trying to safeguard me from being in a situation where temptation could get the better of me.

The Bible warns us to flee temptation. Putting yourself in a position where you must resist temptation is one step closer to falling into sin. Being alone with a member of the opposite sex and having physical contact, particularly with someone you are attracted to, provide too much temptation that you must resist. Although to some this might sound old-fashioned, the truth is never outdated. Romans 13:14 (AMP) teaches us to

make no provision for [indulging] the flesh
[put a stop to thinking about the evil cravings of your physical
nature] to [gratify its] desires (lusts).

It only takes a single moment to give in, but the consequences could last a lifetime. Our inability to live up to a certain standard does not justify lowering the standard. We may struggle to do certain things right, but God will not lower His standard for us. If you develop inner strength, you will be able to handle such challenges and emerge as a champ. I'm not saying you cannot meet up with friends to have fun, but it is best not to knowingly place yourself in a situation where you have to resist temptation.

Another way you allow temptation to enter your life is through your words. What you say has power and can arouse emotions in yourself and in others that could lead to problems. Guard your tongue and you will preserve your strength and your life.

"He who guards his mouth keeps his life,
but he who opens wide his lips comes to ruin"

Proverbs 13:3 (AMP)

As a young person, it is especially important to guard your tongue because there is almost a cultural expectation for young people to talk in obscene and perverse ways, particularly about sex. You should avoid talking about anything that is offensive, indecent, or vulgar, which causes sexual excitement or sparks lustful feelings. It is essential that you guard your tongue and your mind against these things. Profane words do not lead to life. They promote death or a cycle of death and a hollow life based on emotions and feelings rather than on spiritual strength and godly morality.

It's because of this kind of thing that
God is about to explode in anger. It wasn't long ago that you
were doing all that stuff and not knowing any better. But you
know better now, so make sure it's all gone for good: bad temper,
irritability, meanness, profanity, dirty talk.

Colossians 3:8 (MSG)

Beware of humour that employs sexual suggestion or arouses sexual lust. Making a mockery of reproductive body parts or bodily functions in casual talk is an indication of a heart problem. The earlier you deal with it, the better. *Lasciviousness* in Romans 13:13 means disrespectful sexual desire, which is similar to obscenity. Obscene jokes result in lasciviousness when they cause lustful thoughts or improper sexual feelings. We need to detest filthy jesting because it is not only wrong to use filthy language but it is doubly wrong when we derive enjoyment from it and from those who make profane suggestions, even when joking. Think about what you are interested in when no one is watching. Are your thoughts and interests wholesome? Romans 1:32 talks about those who were fully aware of God's penalty for such behaviour but went right on and indulged in these sinful acts and even encouraged others to do so. God will not put up with it, and sin always has consequences.

THE POWER OF YOUR OUTFIT

A few years back, a lady came into my workplace dressed to kill so that everyone in the office was staring at her! Some nearly jumped out of their skin as the lady walked briskly through the open office. My team members began to mumble under their breath. I began to wonder if they knew something about her. So I walked up to my team leader and said, "Is anything wrong?" Two people chorused, "That outfit isn't for a workplace; she must be a call girl."

Your dress or clothing says something to others. It tells others how to address you. Be careful about attracting undue attention to yourself by the way you dress or the way you look. Dress the way you want to be addressed. You are children of the King, so dress like princes and princesses. Dress in a way that reflects your purpose and your worth. It is important that we dress in a way that will not promote lustful thoughts in those around us. We should not be the cause of another's temptation.

It is not acceptable for ladies to indecently expose themselves in order to attract attention. That is the wrong kind of attention anyway! It is wrong for men to take pleasure seeking out and looking at such indecency.

Don't desire her beauty in secret;
don't let her take you in with her eyelashes

Proverbs 6:25 (CEB)

Ladies, your beauty is more than skin deep. True beauty encompasses your behaviour. Although external beauty and trying to enhance your appearance is awesome, perfecting your character is infinitely more important and rewarding.

DON'T BE ALONE

Asking for help when you need it is not a sign of weakness but of strength. True character recognizes the need to seek wisdom and help from others before you can move forward. Do not walk this life alone. To help understand this, we will examine the events surrounding the death of Uriah as described in the Bible. Uriah was a dedicated and loyal man. King David had committed adultery with Uriah's wife, Bathsheba, who became pregnant. In an effort to conceal his sin, David brought Uriah home from the battlefield and told him to go to his wife. David hoped that when Uriah found out about Bathsheba's pregnancy, he would assume the baby to be his own. But Uriah was an honourable man who refused to go home and enjoy the pleasures of married love, knowing that his fellow soldiers were fighting and dying. Thus, he inadvertently disrupted David's cover-up plan. He stayed near King David out of his sense of loyalty and dedication. Desperate to hide his adulterous sin, David sent Uriah back to the battle with a signed letter that was Uriah's death warrant. To cover up his sin, David had Uriah killed. Let's consider what David wrote in the letter:

Put Uriah in the front line of the heaviest fighting and withdraw from him, that he may be struck down and die.

2 Samuel 11:15 (AMP).

David murdered Uriah by ensuring that he would be alone in the thick of the fighting. So, alone and without help, Uriah was killed. Being alone in the midst of any battle such as addiction, masturbation, immoral thoughts, prayerlessness, anger, and so on is a dangerous place to be. You were never meant to fight these battles alone! You need godly people around you to overcome these struggles. Alone, you are more vulnerable because there is no one to help you when you falter, no one to guard your back, no one to help protect you and warn you of dangers you might have overlooked.

Remember, the Bible counsels us not to go to war without wise guidance.

There is safety in many counselors.

Proverbs 24:6

Take advantage of the godly friends and family members whom God has strategically placed around you. With God always on your side, you will not lose a battle! Your victory is guaranteed.

Warmly Yours

THE LORD'S PRAYER CONFESSION

DAILY BENEFITS

The Lord's Prayer 1

Declare by faith and as often as you need

Our Father in Heaven, hallowed be Your name Matthew 6:9

Lord, I come to you as my Father. I thank You because I am your chosen daughter/son. I thank You for forming me and making me in Your image.

Dear Father, I thank You for loving me and for taking me the way I am. You do not just tolerate me but you love me the way I am.

Heavenly Father, I hallow (bless) Your name today. Your name is holy and there is no one else like You.

My father, Your name reflects your holy, loving and merciful nature. I respect and greatly honour Your name. I treat Your name as holy and revere Your name. Therefore, I trust and believe in You.

I believe that You shall look after me today as I go out and come in.

Thank You Father for Your love for me. I thank You for You shall grant me my heart desires in Jesus' name! Amen.

©letterstomyfriendz

DAILY BENEFITS

The Lord's Prayer 2

Declare by faith and as often as you need

Your Kingdom come, Your will be done on earth as it is in Heaven. Matthew 6:10

Dear Father, I desire to do Your will as it is done in Heaven. I therefore ask for the grace to obey You in all things.

Father, You are the only king that reigns in Heaven and on earth. Let Your nature show through every state of affairs in my life. The purpose which You have created me shall be established.

Your life shall reflect in my academics, my relationship, family, my health, career etc.

I shall excel and be outstanding in all things according to Your will.

I stand on your word: whatever does not occur in Heaven shall not be found in me, family and in my environment.

I shall enjoy peace and joy in my life as it is in Heaven.

Evil isn't found in Heaven, no evil shall be traceable to me.

I am victorious in all things in Jesus' name! Amen.

©letterstomyfriendz

DAILY BENEFITS
The Lord's Prayer 3

Give Us This Day Our Daily Bread Matthew 6:11

Dear Father, I thank You for the promise of my daily bread (needs).

Father, I take control of this day by my words. My day is blessed with joy and peace!

Dear God, You shall sustain me physically today. I shall not be weak, lazy or tired to do my daily duties.

I declare that my strength shall not fail me because You shall infuse strength into me.

I step out today in the name of the Lord and I obtain outstanding victory in my work, music, sport, career etc.

I declare that I shall NOT lack good health, friends or relationship, career and good people around me.

I shall not lack good mentors and teachers.

I shall not lack wisdom, knowledge and understanding.

I shall not lack strong mind to make correct decisions.

I receive every good thing that I need to become who You want me to be in Jesus' name! Amen.

©letterstomyfriendz

DAILY BENEFITS
The Lord's Prayer 4
Declare by faith and as often as you need

And forgive us our debts, as we also have forgiven our debtors. Matthew 6:12

Father, I thank You for loving me and sending Your only son to die while I was a sinner.

I acknowledge my short comings today. I pray that You will forgive me all my sins.

You shall purge my conscience from every dead works.

I know You are faithful and just to forgive when I confess; please forgive me of every sin that I have committed intentionally or unintentionally.

The blood of Jesus shall wash me clean as white as snow.

May the words of my mouth and the meditations of my heart be acceptable in Your sight Oh Lord.

I receive the grace to let go of every pain and bitterness in my heart towards my friends, families or neighbours.

I have the heart of Jesus: I will not live in unforgiveness.

I thank You Lord because I am free. I am forgiven. I am a holy child of God! In Jesus' name! Amen.

©letterstomyfriendz

DAILY BENEFITS

The Lord's Prayer 5

Declare by faith and as often as you need

And do not lead us into temptation, but deliver us from the evil one. Matthew 6:13

Father, I thank You because You are always there to lead me in the right path.

I declare today that You shall hold me back from stepping and yielding into temptation.

I shall not walk into evil and evil shall not catch up with me.

The Lord shall deliver me from all forms of evil.

He shall command His angels to guard me in all my ways.

No kidnapper, paedophile or rapist shall come near me because my life is hid in Christ and Christ in God.

Every plan of the devil shall fail concerning me, family and friends.

I shall never go into a wrong and evil relationship.

I shall not be deceived into partaking in anything evil.

I shall never be a victim; I am a conqueror in Jesus' name. Amen.

©letterstomyfriendz

DAILY BENEFITS

The Lord's Prayer 6

Declare by faith and as often as you need

For Yours is the Kingdom and the power and the glory forever. Amen. Matthew 6:13

Dear Lord, I acknowledge Your sovereignty and declare You as Lord in my life today and forever.

I acknowledge that You reign in power and have authority over all things in Heaven and on earth. I recognize that You are everywhere and can do all things. Nothing at all is impossible to You.

I recognize that You are matchless and You reign over all things. All power comes from You for You are the creator of all things.

All that I have and own belongs to You. My beauty, skills, talents and gifts come from You. In You I live, move and have my being.

I give You all the accolade for my achievements and future goals. Your glorious name is magnified in my life today and forever in Jesus' name! Amen.

©letterstomyfriendz

CHAPTER 8

MY THOUGHTS
AT WAR

Dear Friend,

Nothing gives me a headache quite like being lost in silly thoughts. Evil thoughts have the ability to stress and drain your energy, leaving you in fear, guilt, and hopelessness. There was a point in my life when I wished my mother would die – not because I disliked or hated her but because I wanted the pity and attention such a tragedy would bring me. In fact, while my mother was living in England, I told my friends that she had died! How can a Christian descend into such twisted thinking? Yet, I had.

In truth, we all have wrong and silly thoughts that go through our heads at some point. If you walked into any church of any size and asked the congregation if they had ever had evil thoughts flood their minds, if they were honest, every hand would go up. The danger of allowing your thoughts to go wild is that it can jeopardise your relationship with God. God is pure and cannot look at iniquity. If your thoughts are dirty, He cannot relate with you. You need to resist evil thoughts constantly.

[Inasmuch as we] refute arguments and theories and reasonings and every proud and lofty thing that sets itself up against the [true] knowledge of God; and we lead every thought and purpose away captive into the obedience of Christ (the Messiah, the Anointed One).

2 Corinthians 10:5 (AMP)

Do you cast down or rebuke evil or immoral thoughts regularly? Someone has said that a person can dwell so long on a thought that it may take him captive. Martin Luther wrote that evil thoughts are like birds that fly above our heads. We may not be able to stop them flying about, but we certainly can stop them from nesting on our heads! Do not allow wicked thoughts to settle in your mind and heart. Respond as quickly as possible with the Word of God.

When you accept the forgiveness of Christ, you become a citizen of the Kingdom of God. The kingdom of darkness no longer has a hold on you – unless you simply decide to live there. In the Kingdom of God, you have access to supernatural abilities that enable you to take control of your thoughts. You can remove immoral thoughts and fill your heart with wholesome ones.

Do you cast out or rebuke immoral thoughts promptly or just keep quiet and let them fester in your mind? Victory over impure thoughts can be secured by opening your mouth and declaring the Word of God. Don't just think about it, say it loud! Rebuke immoral thoughts. Removing improper thoughts is much more than simply having a New Year's resolution! It is a partnership with the Holy Spirit to allow Him to work in you as you journey unto perfection. God's Word is the best source of direction and wisdom to aid you on this journey. Be aware, however, that the longer those evil thoughts continue, the more deeply they become embedded in your heart and mind. It gets harder and harder to get rid of them, and ultimately you become what you think. This is why it is so important to have the right thoughts.

You were told that your foolish desires will destroy you and that you must give up your old way of life with all its bad habits. Let the Spirit change your way of thinking, and make you into a new person. You were created to be like God, and so you must please him and be truly holy.

Ephesians 4:22-24 (CEB)

I implore you to make an effort to control your thoughts and learn to think about things that are pure, lovely, noble, and of a good report. Proverbs 4:23 encourages you to keep your heart with all diligence, for out of it are the issues of life. What you think determines the way you behave, so protect your mind jealously. Fortunately, regardless of the state of your mind, God is not only willing to work with you, but He knows how to deal with the issues raging through your mind (1 Corinthians 10:13 AMP). However, be aware that controlling your thoughts is your sole responsibility, it not someone else's job. Still, with the help of the Holy Spirit, you can do it! You can cleanse your mind and keep your thoughts pure.

I have strength for all things in Christ who empowers me [I am ready for anything and equal to anything through Him who infuses inner strength into me; I am self-sufficient in Christ's sufficiency].

Philippians 4:13 (AMP)

We are all equal to the task in Christ!

When we commit to changing our minds and our thoughts, we bring pleasure to God. In turn, He instills strength within us to exercise our dominion in the victory that Jesus gave us. Christ's power is inexhaustible! If we pull our strength from Him, we will have an endless supply of strength to resist temptation and persist in keeping our minds pure. Relying on God's Word is the solution!

Now to Him who is able to [carry out His purpose and] do superabundantly more than all that we dare ask or think [infinitely beyond our greatest prayers, hopes, or dreams], according to His power that is at work within us, to Him be the glory in the church and in Christ Jesus throughout all generations forever and ever. Amen.

Ephesians 3:20-21 (AMP)

Warmly Yours

CHAPTER 9

ENERGY BOOSTER

Dear Friend,

Martin Luther recognised the power of God's Word when he said, "All who call on God in true faith, earnestly from the heart, will certainly be heard and will receive what they have asked and desired." To have victory over immoral thoughts, you must give consideration to God's Word.

> *Never stop speaking about this Instruction scroll. Recite it day and night so you can carefully obey everything written in it. Then you will accomplish your objectives, and you will succeed*

Joshua 1:8 (CEB).

The key to victory over immoral thoughts is found in God's Word only. God's Word is essential for spiritual success. Deuteronomy 6:6-9 (CEB) commands us not only to read the Word but to memorise it and recite it to those we have influence over:

> *Talk about them when you are sitting around your house and when you are out and about, when you are lying down and when you are getting up. Tie them on your hand as a sign. They should be on your forehead as a symbol. Write them on your house's doorframes and on your city's gates.*

God wants the truths of His Word to permeate your life, to jog your memory so that you can see them. It is useful to place Bible verses in high-traffic areas of your life such as on your refrigerator, your mirror, your laptop, your TV, and so on. In Matthew 4:1-11, we see that Jesus overcame temptation by using the Scriptures. This strategy worked because He not only had these verses memorized but was able to apply the verses correctly to the situation at hand. You also need to know the Scriptures that you can use throughout each day whenever temptations and situations arise. The following Scriptures and declarations will help you have victory in your thought life.

THE WORD WORKS!

And Jesus, replying, said to them, have faith in God [constantly].
Truly I tell you, whoever says to this mountain, Be lifted up and
thrown into the sea! and does not doubt at all in his heart but
believes that what he says will take place, it will be done for him.
For this reason, I am telling you, whatever you ask for in prayer,
believe (trust and be confident) that it is granted to you,
and you will [get it].

Matthew 21:21 (AMP)

Dear Friend, the battle for your mind rages each and every day so you must equip yourself with Scriptures to prevail in this fight. If evil and immoral thoughts have infiltrated your mind, your thinking will be poisoned and unhealthy. To keep your mind healthy, you must yield it to the Word of God and apply the blood of Jesus to it! Let us confess more of God's Word!

DECLARATIONS

DAILY BENEFITS

The Mind of Christ

Declare by faith & as often as you need

For who has known or understood the mind (the counsels and purposes) of the Lord so as to guide and instruct Him and give Him knowledge? But we have the mind of Christ (the Messiah) and do hold the thoughts (feelings and purposes) of His heart" (1 Corinthians 2: 16).

The Lord shall guide and instruct my mind. The Holy Spirit resides and operates in me, therefore I have the power to think and act according to the word of God. I have a pure heart like Christ. I will think like Jesus, and my thoughts shall be wholesome, pleasing and acceptable to God.

According to Romans 12:2, I submit my life to God, I shall be transformed supernaturally and the things of this world shall no longer have a hold on me. I shall not conform to the world, my mind is renewed and I shall demonstrate the good, acceptable, and perfect will of God in Jesus name! Amen.

©letterstomyfriendz 2015

DAILY BENEFITS

Victory in the Word

Declare by faith and as often as you need

Father, I thank You for Your promises for me in Your Word.
You shall guard my thoughts, my mouth and my actions.
You shall satisfy my needs in drought with all good things.
I shall never experience famine of the Word of God.
You shall satisfy my soul with Your refreshing Word.
Your Word shall dwell richly in me and I shall not sin against You.
Lord, You shall strengthen my bones; You shall keep my soul healthy too.
I shall be like a watered garden; I shall be fresh, beautiful and healthy in my Spirit, soul and body.
I shall be like a spring of water, whose water never goes dry.
I receive continuous guidance from You in Jesus' name! Amen. Isaiah 58:11

©letterstomyfriendz

DAILY BENEFITS

Wholesome thoughts 1

Declare by faith and as often as you need

"For who has known or understood the mind (the counsels and purposes) of the Lord so as to guide and instruct Him and give Him knowledge? But we have the mind of Christ (the Messiah) and do hold the thoughts (feelings and purposes) of His heart." (1 Corinthians 2: 16) The Lord shall guide and instruct my mind. The Holy Spirit resides and operates in me. Therefore, I have the power to think and act according to the Word of God. I have a pure heart like Christ. I will think like Jesus, and my thoughts shall be wholesome, pleasing and acceptable to God.
According to Romans 12:2, I submit my life to God, I shall be transformed supernaturally and the things of this world shall no longer have a hold on me. I shall not conform to the principles of the world, my mind is renewed and I shall demonstrate the good, acceptable, and perfect will of God in Jesus' name! Amen.

©letterstomyfriendz

DAILY BENEFITS

Wholesome thoughts 2

Declare by faith and as often as you need

I overcome Satan by the blood of the Lamb and by the word of my testimony (Revelation 12:11). I triumph over every evil thought by the power of the Holy Spirit. I cleanse my spirit, soul and body by the blood of the Lamb. "The words of my mouth and the meditations of my heart shall be pleasing to You, Lord, my rock and my redeemer". (Psalm 19:14)
I am washed and set free by the blood of Jesus. My thoughts from now on shall be healthy. I am Jesus' bride and the Holy Spirit is at work in me to present me to the father without spot and wrinkle. I receive liberty to think wholesomely and I receive answers to my prayers with joy and thanksgiving in Jesus' name! Amen.

©letterstomyfriendz

Consider these Bible verses:

...having our hearts sprinkled and purified from a guilty (evil) conscience and our bodies cleansed with pure water

Hebrews 10:22 (AMP)

What is the pure water? It is the Word of God

Ephesians 5:26

Don't get bogged down in the Word of God, don't get bored, and don't give up. Stay in the Word and soak it up! The Word of God is the instruction book for life. If we are to journey through this life and all the obstacles therein, then our victory can only be guaranteed by the Word.

HAVE A PLAN

Those who achieve success do so because they have a plan and execute that plan. The same is true in your life. If you intend to succeed in your thought life, you need a specific, practical checklist of steps you are going to take to achieve victory:

Step 1: Recognise the importance of getting rid of immoral thoughts. There are awesome rewards and benefits which include a complete transformation not only on the outside but on the inside, too. You will also enjoy the benefit of knowing and understanding the will of God for your life.

Step 2: Examine the conditions or circumstances that seem to weaken your mind, that is, that influence you to accept and dwell on immoral or evil thoughts.

Step 3: Prepare a plan that will allow you either to avoid those situations or to fight them if you cannot avoid them. Write your plan down and even share it with others. No one plans to fail, but we often fail because we do not plan. Part of your plan must include studying and memorising the Word of God.

Nature abhors a vacuum. It is not enough to try to rid yourself of evil thoughts; you must put righteous thoughts in their place. Otherwise, those evil thoughts will come back. For example, suppose you determine to spend less time on social networking sites, and you put your phone down, determined you are not going to pick it up or look at it even if it vibrates with an incoming notification. With nothing else to do, however, it may be difficult to take your mind away from the phone. Soon the temptation becomes overwhelming, and you may succumb unless you find something productive to do. Instead of just sitting idle, pick up a book and begin reading, take a long walk and pray, play a sport; find something constructive ways to engage your mind.

Step 4: Recognise that you are a spirit and that you are in charge of what you think. A thought has no control over you other than the power you give it. You can exercise your dominion, and when you do, your victory is certain!

These are practical ways to come out victorious.

THE RIGHT KIND OF TALK

Talk is good – if you are talking to the right person and utilizing the right words. Remember that life and death are in the power of the tongue (Proverbs 18:31). It is clear that our words have power both to do great good and to do great harm. God created the universe by merely speaking it into existence. So, too, our minds are sustained and powered by the words we speak and the words we hear and heed.

One key essential aspect of talking is prayer. Prayer is talking to God. Prayer is the means by which we exercise our authority to establish the will of God here on earth. We must pray on a regular basis if we desire victory in our minds (1 Thessalonians 5:17).

I encourage you to pray especially at the moments when you face temptations or challenges. Whenever your mind is weak and susceptible, you must fortify it through prayer. Unless you have formed a habit of prayer, however, your mind may not turn to God in such times. No wonder Jesus said, "Stay awake and pray that you won't be tested. You want to do what is right, but you are weak" (Matthew 26:41).

You may recall that Jesus' disciples were in that situation of not being able to stay awake at a pivotal moment in Jesus' life and their own lives. You would think that witnessing Jesus' agony in the garden and facing Judas' imminent betrayal would make them pray more, but it wasn't so. They fell asleep three times despite Jesus' pleadings with them to pray with Him. It is wise to take the time to get in the habit of prayer while you are fresh and awake. That way, when your mind is under attack, you will fall back upon that which you are in the habit of doing –praying!

YOU ARE ASSURED!

God has promised that if you ask for help, He will hear and answer.
Casting the whole of your care [all your anxieties, all your worries,
your concerns, once and for all] on Him, for He cares for you
affectionately and cares about you watchfully.

1 Peter 5:7 (AMP)

Don't ever do the "worrying" by yourself. Give it to a specialist who is adequate to handle it. It doesn't matter what situation you are worried about – whether with your heart, relationship, studies, family or friends – give it to Him. God is able to make your heart whole and grant you joy.

In the fight against immoral thoughts and desires, it may help to choose one or two spiritually mature friends to talk to on a regular basis. It will help to share Bible passages with each other, to listen to their spiritual wisdom and encouraging words, and to let their scriptural advice guide you and effect change in your situation. Often, it is encouraging just to know that you are not the only person in a battle. You have a comrade, a fellow soldier to fight along with you and to "have your back." It is a blessing not only to receive this help but to give it to another believer who is engaging in the battle. Helping others overcome their spiritual battles strengthens you to fight your own. Indeed, having people you can pray with is very special and important.

Cristy Lane recorded a song called *One Day At a Time* (United Artists Records, 1980), written by Country and Western songwriters Marijohn Wilkin and Kris Kristofferson. Part of the lyrics said:

One day at a time, sweet Jesus

That's all I'm asking from you.

Just give me the strength

To do every day what I have to do.

Yesterday's gone, sweet Jesus

And tomorrow may never be mine.

Lord, help me today, show me the way

One day at a time.

Don't worry about tomorrow. You have enough things to deal with today (Matthew 6:33-34). Don't allow yourself to get so overwhelmed with future issues and overcoming temptations that you just want to quit. All you need to focus on is doing right today – just today! You can do that. Each morning when you get up, it is a brand-new day. Promise yourself and God that you will meditate on His Word for strength to get through that day. Tomorrow will come, and when it does, it will be today, and you will deal with it – one day at a time.

An older friend visited my house when I was newly married and mentioned that my clean house would be difficult to maintain once we had children. She wondered how I would cope with the mess of children because I was so meticulous in my cleaning. I calmly replied, "One day at a time." I just need to enjoy today. Tomorrow and its temptations and struggles will come, but all I need to focus on is today. This is also the way to walk with God.

My favourite Bible verse when I was in secondary school was Galatians 6:9 (CEB): "Let's not get tired of doing good because in time we'll have a harvest if we don't give up." It was such a great consolation to know that my commitment towards living holy would not go unrecognised. I found comfort in knowing that I would be compensated if I continued to do well. You may struggle with immoral thoughts but just keep confessing the Word. Do not give up. According to Peter 3:18, becoming a mature Christian is a process of growth. You are born again spiritually as a baby and gradually grow up in Christ. Do not be impatient with yourself. This process takes time.

I was shocked recently when I saw a picture of myself when I was in university. I could not believe how young I looked then and how much older I look now. My friends said they didn't recognise much change in me until they saw the pictures from my university days. The changes were profound. In the same way, although you may not see much change in your thoughts immediately when comparing today to yesterday, if you diligently apply the principles that God's Word teaches, you will see significant changes over time as compared to when you began.

Warmly Yours

Passing Notes Between God and Me:

1. The godly qualities I desire:
2. I desire a change in these areas:
3. I will avoid these immoral thought triggers:
4. Relevant Bible passages about the changes I desire:

Meditate on these verses daily and fill your mind with them.

CHAPTER 10

THE MORE WE CHAT, THE CLOSER WE BECOME

Dear Friend,

Some years ago, I met a friendly guy who seemed to share my Christian faith. We hit it off right away. It was as if we had known each other our entire lives. We talked extensively as comfortably as if we were old friends. I thought I had found another good Christian friend, but something in me warned me that things were not right.

> *Spiritual people comprehend everything,*
> *but they themselves aren't understood by anyone.*
>
> 1 Corinthians 2:15 (CEB).

It occurred to me that this guy wanted something more than a godly friendship. I knew the relationship was going in the wrong direction and that I needed to break off my friendship with him. Although we hardly saw each other in person, it was still very difficult to let it go since we had grown close through our daily talks. I hope this will serve as a warning to you. Anyone you spend that much time talking with will become very dear to your heart, and even when you realise that something is wrong, you may be so emotionally attached that backing out will be difficult. I found this out the hard way.

So, determined to keep things pure and holy, I decided to call off the friendship. I felt I owed him some explanation, so I decided to explain what the Bible says about immorality. I was fooling myself! Each time I spoke to him, he would counter what I said with different Bible passages. This just prolonged our conversations. I prayed and was honest with God about my feelings, and He confirmed that the association was wrong.

God kept working with me very gently and gave me Scriptures to instruct me. Eventually, I found a way of escape. The answer is so obvious – and probably obvious to you, too: I simply stopped talking to him. As time went on, the emotional connection began to dissipate. I refused to respond to any of his various attempts at communication. I was tempted to respond with Scripture, but even that was a trap because once I started communication, I knew that it would not stop. Finally, he gave up, and I was delivered from that ungodly friendship.

Reflecting on that situation and thinking from another angle, the more we communicate with God, the closer we will become to Him. When we stop communicating with God, the closeness will begin to wane. If we truly want to keep our relationship with God strong, we need to be in constant fellowship with Him.

ENJOYING PRAYER

Remember that prayer is communicating with your Heavenly Father. In every type of communication, there must be a transmitter and a receiver. You transmit, and God receives. You may not know whether your prayers are received, however, unless there is some response or a witness in your heart. God conveys messages, but you must train your spirit to grasp those messages by meditating and practicing the Word of

God. You must stop to listen after talking to God to develop your ability to hear His voice.

Listening truly is a skill that you can acquire both in your natural relationships and in your relationship with God. God's messages or instructions open your inner eyes to learn and see things differently. This is called revelation. God speaks and reveals many things through His Word.

It is vital that we tune our ears to hear God. If Abraham had not been willing to hear from God, he would have killed his much-loved son, Isaac. When you pray, you must expect to receive something from God. On the other hand, prayer is more than just asking for and receiving things from God. It is a spiritual communion with God in worship, supplication, thanksgiving, adoration, and confession. It is a way for you to relate and fellowship with God. Prayer can be an enjoyable time, a way to bond with God, and it does not have to be formal. You can have communion with God anywhere, anytime, and in a way that reflects your personality. You see, God wants to be friends with you, and you can connect with Him when you pray.

> *I don't call you servants any longer, because servants don't know what their master is doing. Instead, I call you friends, because everything I heard from my Father I have made known to you.*

John 15:15

As a young person, you are happy and comfy to talk with someone you consider to be your best friend. In fact, you will ignore other important things just to talk to this person. You can get so caught up in your time together that you don't even realise how much time has passed. This is what your prayer life should become. When you and God enjoy being with each other so much, time will just pass without realisation. This is something He yearns for. I am striving to attain this goal. If you desire it, too, then we can work and walk together.

The book of Genesis is clear about why God created man. Genesis 1:28 (CEB) states:

God blessed them and said to them, 'Be fertile and multiply;
fill the earth and master it. Take charge of the fish of the sea,
the birds in the sky, and everything crawling on the ground.

God meant for man to have dominion over God's creation. Beyond that, God wanted intimate fellowship with man. Fellowship is defined as a friendly, compassionate relationship. God wanted companions with a free will who could choose to love Him.

Genesis 3:8 (CEB) shows God's heart: "during that day's cool evening breeze, they heard the sound of the LORD God walking in the garden." God took pleasure in Adam's company. Unfortunately, when man disobeyed God and ate of the forbidden fruit, that fellowship was broken. The broken fellowship was repaired when Jesus died on the Cross as the second Adam and reconciled us back to God (1 Corinthians 15:45).

It is no news to say that Adam and Eve are no longer here, but God continues to search for people who want to fellowship with Him. Is that person you?

Look! I'm standing at the door and knocking.
If any hear my voice and open the door, I will come in to be with
them, and will have dinner with them, and they will have dinner
with me... If you can hear, listen to what the
Spirit is saying to the churches.

Revelation 3:19-22 (CEB)

Companionship entails many things, but the primary ingredient is spending time with each other. Can you recall that guy or girl you fancied so much? Do you recall how you would go out of your way to spend time with him or to talk with her? Being in the presence of God should be similar. It can bring even more joy and peace than you can imagine. Jesus maintained constant fellowship with God while here on Earth.

A constant worry I had as a young believer was that I found it difficult to spend twenty minutes in fellowship with God. I really wanted to know God, but despite my zeal I would only spend around ten minutes a day with Him. Jesus, however, went to a mountain alone and spent the entire night in fellowship with God. I often wondered how Jesus could do that.

I used to write down different things to pray about just to force myself to pray longer, but I would run through my prayer topics in under ten minutes. Jesus didn't need that, but for me, prayer was like a big burden because I did not know what to say during prayer like others who prayed for a whole hour or more. I was not aware that prayer was about being in the presence of the only God who loves me, and experiencing the richness of joy that His presence could bring. I believe Jesus was not only making requests but also expressing His love for God. He spent time getting to know His Father. When you pray, you can also share your thoughts, needs, and desire to do His will.

Prayer is not all about asking for things that you need. Fellowship with God is an experience beyond requests. It is a lifestyle of desiring to be in the company of someone who loves you most. I enjoy catching up with friends after a time of separation. Many of my childhood friends are married now, so it is harder to talk the entire night away as we once did. When we do find the time to get together, however, the hours seem to fly by like minutes. When you become lost in the joy of being in the presence of God, the closeness you experience causes the time to fly by.

I was part of the *Workers in Training* Program at my local church. As part of that training, we were encouraged to spend one hour in prayer each day. I struggled with that – not with the length of time but with trying to find the time. Then it dawned on me that I didn't struggle to find time to spend with my friends. It was easy to spend an hour on the phone with them, and yet I was struggling to find the time to spend with the One who loves my soul. This should not be happening. God longs for fellowship with us. Every believer needs to decide to have quality time with God, which starts with a desire to be with Him. God knows your heart and is able to grant you this desire.

The Psalmist declared in Psalm 27:4 (CEB),

I have asked one thing from the Lord— it's all I seek: to live in the Lord's house all the days of my life, seeing the Lord's beauty and constantly adoring his temple.

David's longing was granted. Indeed, God called David a man after His own heart. I cannot imagine the depth of the relationship David had with God that made him so excited that he craved to be in the presence of God forever. David must have experienced something very dynamic and remarkable in God's presence. If God granted David's desire, He will grant yours!

Like David, don't just ask things from God when you are in His presence. Praise Him! Worship Him! Let your heart sing out to Him! So often, the time we spend with God is one-sided, and we do not let our hearts become full with Him. Psalm 27 declares who the Lord was to David. Who is God to you? You can declare who the Lord is to you confidently in prayers. Psalm 27 also speaks of safety in the presence of God, but we will find more than protection. We will also find advancement, joy, forgiveness, answers to questions, and physical and spiritual strength in the presence of God, but to obtain these things we must be in His presence!

If you find it difficult to spend more than five minutes in prayer, try writing a letter to God. While writing, you will discover that you have more and more to talk to God about. Writing can develop and strengthen your fellowship with God. Also, those letters can become a record of some of the wonderful things God has done for you!

Ephesians 3:14-21 declares our need to be totally reliant upon God. One of the reasons we bow in prayer is to show our humility and dependence on Him. When we become dependent upon God, we give Him control over every aspect of our lives. We let Him become responsible for our welfare.

Surrendering to God according to the passage above is a conscious and deliberate act. No one surrenders to Him by accident. It must be a calculated decision. If you really want an intimate relationship with God, you must make a conscious effort. You need to take action. You have talked about praying long enough. Now it is time to do it – to begin praying. So choose a time and a place to do it and begin. Remember, you don't do good and right things by accident; you do them on purpose. You plan to do right and then follow through.

TAKE TIME OUT

I came from a large family, so I was rarely alone. When I moved to the United Kingdom away from many of my family members, I struggled to adjust to the fact that I did not have a close family member, friend, or neighbour around all the time. In the UK, everyone seemed too busy and serious to stop and just be friendly. People hardly even said, "Hello," and I considered leaving the country several times because of that. How can people get so involved in their routines that they do not take time out to be friendly? I cried and felt completely alone when no one took the time to knock on my door and ask how I was doing.

I truly struggled with feeling all alone. I tried to get others to join me in prayer, singing, and fasting. I didn't want to do these things alone because I was used to doing them with family members and friends. I enjoyed worshiping God with others, but what I discovered was that true spiritual growth takes place not in the company of others but in being alone with God. The truth is that to truly enjoy God as you should, you need to learn to be alone with Him. Although other people have their places in our life, we must take time out to get to know God, and this will not happen until you can get alone with Him. You must take time out from your busy schedule and all the distractions the world offers. Although it is true that the Bible teaches us that there are a time and a place for fellow believers to unite in prayer, much more so, we need to get alone with God so we can truly get to know Him.

It is in your prayer closet when it is just you and God that you are most honest in your prayers. There, alone with God, your heart does not worry about what others think of you. Your prayers become more than mere words. They become an expression of who you are and who God is to you. Treasure your time alone with God, for in this quietness, you will hear His voice clearly and find peace, direction, comfort, and victory in your life.

Warmly Yours

Notes

As a child of God, it is important that you have several ways of expressing yourself to God. Think of what works for you and ask God for a consistent spirit so that you will communicate with Him daily.

Planning to connect with God every day

Time:

Prayer topics:

How:

Here are a few suggestions to help you connect with Him.

1. Study Psalm 136, which describes everything God has done because He loves us dearly. Think about your life and list some things that have happened to you. Follow each occurrence, positive and negative, with "for His love endures forever."
2. Meditate and proclaim some intense hymns: *Take my life and let it be*, *Now thank we all our God* and *It is well with my soul* (just to mention a few).
3. Play and sing your favourite worship songs.
4. Write a letter to God. Express your gratitude to God in writing.
5. Talk to God about everything that happened during the day.
6. Choose a Bible passage and reflect on it. Replace worry or negative thought with a Scripture. Think hard about the verse until it has accomplished the purpose …

CHAPTER 11

ALL GAIN, NO LOSS

Dear Friend,

I really hate failing. In fact, my fear of failure was very high when I was a teenager. I struggled with my academics and even convinced myself that some people were just never ever going to be good enough. I thought I was in that category. When I became a Christian, however, I began to listen to teachings on prayer and to study what the Word of God said about success. When I began to apply these principles and confess the Word to strengthen my heart, I made great strides in my academic endeavours. Those prayers did not go to waste!

At the end of my days at university, I took a final exam that would determine whether or not I would graduate. I turned in the exam, hoping I had done well. I knew, however, that I had not put in as much time as I should have, and it bothered me the whole time I was on holiday. On the day I was to find out whether I had passed, I had a dream that I had failed one of the subjects and would not be able to graduate. In my dream, I saw five students pleading with the professor to bring my score up to a passing grade. When I woke up, I began to pray and cancelled the dream in the name of Jesus. I immediately rushed back to the school. Three of my friends and two others in the class began to comfort me. They had found out I had not passed the exam and would not graduate with them.

My dream had come true. My mind went blank. I did not know what to do or say. The lecturer, who was known for delighting in a student's failure, would not budge. I went back to a friend, and we began to pray. She reminded me of prayers we had sown into our future. So we prayed more earnestly until about 11:00 p.m. The following morning, I went back to the school and walked around the department, unsure what to do. As I stood in front of the lecturer's office, I felt the need to go in and speak to him. So I walked in and told him that I had failed his course.

He looked at me and smiled scornfully. I didn't know what to say, so I asked him if I could see my papers. I remember scoring 20/30 in the continuous assessment test the lecturer had administered earlier in the semester and wondered how I could have possibly scored 16/70 (22.9%) on the final exam that translated into the 36% he had recorded against my name! Happily, when I saw my exam script, I saw that I had scored 36/70. With tears of joy streaming down my face, I pointed out to him that he had not added the 20 marks I scored in the test to the exam score of 36 in his computation, which would have brought my overall score to 56%. Staring right into my eyes, he said, "Have you been praying? You would have failed if your God had not directed you here at this time." Yippee! I graduated.

Remember that I had already invested prayers into the future. God would not let those prayers be in vain. I pray that you, too, will discover this power in prayer. If you pray, the Lord will see to it that your prayers are not in vain. Someone said that we are who and what we are because of our prayer lives. The shallower you are in prayer, the weaker you will be in resisting the devil. The more you pray, the deeper your spiritual roots will delve and the stronger you will become. To grow in righteousness, you will need to sink your roots deeper in prayers and in God's Word. Spiritual maturity does not happen by accident. You must do whatever it takes to achieve it. You have nothing to lose when you pray.

CLOSE CALLS WITH RAPE

I recall a time when I woke up and could not recall a dream I had the night before. I knew only that I had dreamt; I could not remember what the dream was about. As I was praying that morning, I had a strange feeling that I needed to pray against being raped. Although I could not explain the feeling, I prayed for God's protection and made sure that I avoided walking alone at night. Rapists, however, do not operate only at night.

A few days later, one of my sisters sent me on an errand to pick up something she wanted to borrow from a male friend of hers. I knocked on the door but got no response. I heard something and turned around to see his younger brother come rushing across the street to open the door for me.

When he invited me in, I told him I was in a hurry and just wanted the cassette tape I had come to pick up for my sister. He moved as if he intended to go inside and call for his brother, but then he suddenly grabbed me from behind. Terrified, I struggled to get him to let go of me. He said, "You parade about like you are a virgin, but today I will find out!" He pushed me into a room where I began to scream and shout for help, not knowing that his brother was not in the house. Only his aged and visually impaired grandmother was in the house.

Though I was shouting the name of Jesus, he took no heed. I became dizzy, disoriented in my fear. I recall asking, "Do you really want to do this?" He pinned my arms behind me and grabbed my dress. Desperately, I shouted that I needed water. He hesitated, figuring he could grant this request before I could escape. In the brief time he was away, I managed to find a glass bottle I could use to defend myself.

When he came back, I brandished the bottle in his face, screaming, "If you come near me, I'll do something nasty!" We exchanged threats as I inched towards the door. Finally close enough, I lunged for the door and escaped, running as fast as my legs could carry me. I kept this terrifying event to myself, not wanting to hurt my sister who was a close friend of my attacker's older brother. I sometimes wonder what might have occurred if I had not prayed for protection against rape. I will always be grateful to God for helping me to escape the snare of the enemy.

Dear Friend, I barely escaped being raped on four different occasions when I was a teenager. Although that may sound like a lot and is very scary, let it serve as a warning and a reminder that it still happens today. I can assure you that all my escapes were strictly God's intervention. In fact, God revealed two of these incidents to me in advance.

Rape is evil that stems from the heart. Take this godly counsel from me. You may want to read the chapter *My Thoughts at War* again. You need to do all you can to guard against silly thoughts and lustful imaginings. Guys, rape and other coerced sexual activity are not excusable; they are not youthful exuberance. They are pure evil!

Listen to me. Here is the truth: Ladies do not get raped because they wear suggestive clothing or drink or are under the influence of drugs. Ladies do not get raped because they walk alone in the park or are not careful enough. Ladies get raped because guys let their thoughts run wild and are careless and unable to control their thoughts with the Word of God. Friends, don't let emotions dictate your behaviour. Boost your spiritual energy because you will need your stamina to resist the suggestions of the devil. Let your spirit dictate your actions; give no room for your flesh.

GOD REVEALED A MAJOR SECRET TO DANIEL THROUGH PRAYER

God revealed a major secret to Daniel and his friends in Daniel chapter 2. The king made an impossible demand of Daniel and his friends. The king wanted someone to reveal and interpret his dream – a dream he had entirely forgotten himself. The Chaldeans (astrologers and astronomers who lived in southern Babylonia, which today is the southern part of Iraq) were confused and said:

No one on earth can do what the king is asking

Daniel 2:10 (CEB).

What the king was asking was simply not possible! So Daniel went home and asked his three friends to ask the God of heaven for help about this mystery, in hopes that Daniel and his friends wouldn't die with the rest of Babylon's sages. Then, in a vision by night, the mystery was revealed to Daniel! Daniel praised the God of heaven. Daniel 2:18-19 (CEB).

Those four men decided to call upon God, and as a result, they received the interpretation to King Nebuchadnezzar's dream and their lives were spared. Prayer will redeem your life from destruction and also reveal great mysteries. You see? When we pray, God reveals the enemy's plans and intervenes on our behalf. It is during prayer that His will is revealed to us, too. Prayers are very effective, so do not forget to take the time to pray!

Warmly Yours

CHAPTER 12

THE RIGHT PRAYER

Dear Friend,

Some of my friends are honest enough to admit that they struggle to pray for more than ten minutes at a time. That was true for me when I was younger. When the church gathered for prayer, I was always the first person to finish. I always wondered what others were praying about that took so long! Eventually, the Lord revealed a secret to prayer that changed my life.

God revealed to me that He answers through His Word, so I then began to pray the Word. For example, if I wanted to spend time praising God, I would use my own words but then read Psalms 21, 100, 134, and 136. I would thank Him as I read these chapters verse by verse. The book of Psalms is full of praise and thanksgiving. After praising Him, I would ask for forgiveness by reading a few verses of the Scriptures. In a short time, I had these passages memorised and could quote them as I prayed. As time went on, I was praying for an hour at a time with no problems at all! I often spent the whole hour just thanking and praising Him and never getting around to making requests.

By praying the Word, you will notice a significant change in your spiritual life. It will bring maturity and revelation. Even as a young person, you will begin to discern the will of God for your life. You will be conforming to the Word of God as you continually draw closer to Him, and you will gain understanding and discernment.

Prayer is the avenue through which we claim the promises that God has given to us in His Word. Labouring in prayer is taking hold of God – much as Jacob did when he wrestled with the angel all night – to receive His blessings. God wants nothing more than for us to lay hold of His Word and give Him free reign in our lives to fulfil His promises.

My Dear Friend, what things has God has promised you in His Word? Claim them in prayers. Victory over sin is found in the pages of the Bible! Take hold of the Word and claim the blessings that God has already set aside for you! You can live a holy life. You can break that sinful habit. You can be victorious in your prayer life. So many promises are within the Word of God just waiting for you to lay claim to them through prayer. If you can grasp this truth, it will change your life. Daniel illustrated this truth:

> *In the first year of his reign, I, Daniel, understood from the books the number of years which, according to the word of the Lord to Jeremiah the prophet, must pass by before the desolations [which had been] pronounced on Jerusalem should end; and it was seventy years. And I set my face to the Lord God to seek Him by prayer and supplications, with fasting and sackcloth and ashes.*

Daniel 9:2-3 (AMP)

God can do anything when His children decide to pray. When we humble ourselves and seek God's intervention in the nation in which we live, God will answer us. He will renew our strength according to His Word in Isaiah 40:28-31. The truth is, you might not feel like praying, and sometimes when you do pray you may feel like nothing is happening. But every time you pray, you are definitely generating energy. Prayers release strength.

JESUS' MODEL FOR PRAYER

Prayer is not all about me, myself, and I. Prayer should not be selfish. When Jesus taught His disciples to pray, He gave them a model for their prayers. Jesus was praying, and when He finished, one of his disciples said, "Lord, teach us to pray, just as John taught his disciples" (Luke11:1 CEB). He gave them this illustration:

> *He also said to them, "Imagine that one of you has a friend and*
> *you go to that friend in the middle of the night. Imagine saying,*
> *'Friend, loan me three loaves of bread because a friend of mine on a*
> *journey has arrived and I have nothing to set before him.'*
> *Imagine further that he answers from within the house,*
> *'Don't bother me. The door is already locked, and my children*
> *and I are in bed. I can't get up to give you anything.' I assure you,*
> *even if he wouldn't get up and help because of his friendship, he will*
> *get up and give his friend whatever he needs because of his friend's*
> *boldness. And I tell you: Ask and you will receive. Seek and you will*
> *find. Knock and the door will be opened to you."*

Luke 11:5-9 (CEB)

Prayer is not only for your personal needs. In the example above, Jesus described intercessory prayer, which is praying on behalf of someone else. Think about these:

"A friend of mine on a journey has arrived" (Luke 11:6a). Prayer can meet the needs of others!

The disciples said, "Teach us how to pray" (Luke11:1b). Prayer can be taught. Identify a mature Christian who can teach and encourage you to pray. Pray for your family members, friends, and neighbours who are not Christians. Pray for the Church, missionaries, the community, troubled nations, and so on. Shift attention away from yourself and take up another person's burden in prayer. By doing this, you will find joy in that you are blessing others. Indeed, you will enjoy prayer all the more.

Warmly Yours

Notes

Identify individuals or a community whom you want to pray for.

1. Name:
   Needs:

2. Name:
   Needs:

3. Name:
   Needs:

CHAPTER 13

LESSONS FROM NATURE

Dear Friend,

We can gain insight into our spiritual growth by learning valuable lessons from nature. The beauty of God's creation is everywhere, and trees are a major part of what God has made. From the deep and powerful roots to the massive trunk that stands tall and mighty to the supple branches that spread overhead to the fruit that brings sustenance – trees exude life. There is an astounding variety of trees, small and big, wide and thin, evergreens and fruit trees. Even the fruit they bear varies. Some trees produce sweet, succulent fruit while others produce bitter, tart fruit. Trees provide shade during hot days and shelter on rainy days.

So, yes, the tree is a significant part of God's creation, but where do they gain their strength? The answer is simple: from their roots. Dear Friend, once we identify where our strength lies, other things will fall into place. You need to establish a firm foundation so the structure can remain strong and secure. For a believer to be strong, he or she must have roots that are firmly planted in God and in His Word. Let's examine the roots of a tree. For a tree to stand tall, it must have roots that are grounded properly. These roots do not just appear. They grow down over time and with effort.

Compare your life to that of a tree. How is your root system? Are your roots grounded, allowing you to bring forth the fruit of the Spirit? The fruit of the Spirit (singular, not plural, as it is one fruit with many aspects) is love, joy, peace, patience, kindness, goodness, faithfulness, gentleness and self-control. Although when we look at a tree, we do not see the roots, we do see the effects of what the roots do. The deeper the roots, the healthier and stronger the tree; the shallower the roots, the weaker the tree. If we are going to produce godly fruit in our lives, we must have strong spiritual roots.

Trees with weak root systems are more susceptible to powerful winds and storms. Although the storm may sway trees with deep roots, once the storm has passed, the trees remain standing strong. That is true for Christians. Storms of life will come our way, and if we intend to weather them, we must have a strong root system.

Hear what Jesus said:

> *I am the True Vine, and My Father is the Vinedresser.*
> *Any branch in Me that does not bear fruit [that stops bearing)*
> *He cuts away (trims off, takes away); and He cleanses and*
> *repeatedly prunes every branch that continues to bear fruit, to make*
> *it bear more and richer and more excellent fruit. You are cleansed*
> *and pruned already, because of the word which I have given you*
> *[the teachings I have discussed with you]. Dwell in me, and I will*
> *dwell in you. [Live in me, and I will live in you.] Just as no branch*
> *can bear fruit of itself without abiding in (being vitally united to)*
> *the vine, neither can you bear fruit unless you abide in Me.*
> *I am the Vine; you are the branches. Whoever lives in me and*
> *I in him bears much (abundant) fruit. However, apart from me*
> *[cut off from vital union with me] you can do nothing.*

John 15:1-8 (AMP)

Jesus told us to abide in Him. We must stay with Him and continue in Him so that we will stay alive. Our spiritual lives have purpose beyond merely growing. We are to reproduce – to bring forth fruit. That only happens when we have an intimate relationship with Jesus Christ. That relationship is more than merely attending church services and being active in the choir or any other voluntary departments in the church. To remain or abide in Christ is to continue to grow in our personal relationship with God. There is no turning back! God is perfectly functional and independent of us, but we need Him if we are to function as He intended us to.

IT MAY HURT

I once watched a video on how to prune vines. I noticed that the plant was difficult to maintain and rather touchy. To produce a quality crop, the husbandman must give the vine serious attention. And it takes quite a bit of pruning for a grapevine to produce a larger crop. You need approximately ten shoots with at least two buds on each. As for the rest of the new growth, it must be cut off, which is an essential part of cultivating the vine. This is the key element that will determine whether the vine will produce a healthy and large harvest.

Without this knowledge, you might suspect that the husbandman was abusing the vine with his vigorous pruning, which is essential to better growth. If there are too many shoots, the new growth will siphon off important nutrients that should go into producing grapes. The pruning process ensures that growth and fruit production are guided properly and that growth does not happen haphazardly. In the Kingdom of God, abiding and pruning are keys to bearing much fruit. Pruning (correction) is part of your journey with God. When God instructs or reproves you, be quick to act upon His guidance!

How willing are you to take correction? Know this: Those who can take correction will find their roots strengthened and will bear much fruit. If you want nutrients, you must continue to remain connected to Him. The branches of a grapevine have little value aside from the fruit they produce. People don't cultivate grapevines for the wood but only for the grapes. We are the branches, and if we want to have eternal value, we must abide in the vine – Jesus Christ.

If you don't remain in me, you will be like a branch that is thrown out and dries up. Those branches are gathered up, thrown into a fire, and burned. If you remain in me and my words remain in you, ask for whatever you want and it will be done for you. My Father is glorified when you produce much fruit and in this way prove that you are my disciples.

John 15:6 (CEB)

Friends, your strength lies in a consistent relationship with God. Let me share some tips that have helped me develop a steady and consistent fellowship with Him.

1. Connect with God early in the morning before you get distracted with other things.
2. Become a student of the Word. The Word of God holds the answers to the questions of your heart.
3. Find someone who has a steady relationship with God to help you grow.
4. Talk to God about all things and practice your listening skills. Be conscious of His presence all the time.
5. Regularly reflect on your relationship with God. Be honest with yourself and open up to God. Are you standing in Christ? Are you making progress or following the crowd? Do you need to return to God? Examine your heart and make a decision to give God the best of your years.

Warmly Yours

CHAPTER 14

THE ULTIMATE ENERGY BOOSTER

Dear Friend,

Let's talk about a life of worship. "Church is boring … just unexciting!" or "Well, church is all about *dos* and *don'ts*. I've just lost interest in the things of God." I hear a few of my friends in church say such things. Can you identify with those feelings? Is there a spiritual emptiness inside that you cannot fill up? Is there something missing in your relationship with God? Is it hard for you to experience the joy of His presence as the Psalmist described in Psalm 16:9-11?

> *Therefore my heart is glad, and my whole being rejoices;*
> *my flesh also dwells secure. For you will not abandon my soul to*
> *Sheol, or let your holy one see corruption. You make known to me*
> *the path of life; in your presence there is fullness of joy;*
> *at your right hand are pleasures forevermore.*

If you are feeling unenthusiastic and unexcited about your relationship with God, know that you are not alone. Many others feel the same way, but there is a solution. There is healing when we worship.

When Jesus spoke to the woman at Jacob's well, He revealed an eternal truth that every Christian needs to grasp. He said,

*A time will come, however, indeed it is already here, when the
true (genuine) worshipers will worship the Father in Spirit and in
truth (reality); for the Father is seeking just such people as these as
His worshipers. God is a Spirit (a spiritual Being) and those who
worship Him must worship Him in spirit and in truth.*

John 4:23-26 (AMP)

We receive revelations and inspirations when we worship from the
heart. The questions of our hearts are answered in true worship. In verse
10 of this same Bible passage, Jesus revealed to her what she did not know:

*... If you knew the gift of God and who it is that asks
you for a drink, you would have asked him and he would
have given you living water.*

Jesus also told the woman all she ever done and introduced Himself
to her: "the one speaking to you – I am he." What a joy to worship!

I was a member of the choir for many years, and my understanding
of worship was simply singing a few slow-rhythm songs while raising
my hands. That was only partially true. There are many biblical Hebrew
words for praise and worship for which the meaning was simply
translated as *praise* in English versions of the Bible. *Halal*, the base word
in hallelujah, is a celebration of worship to boast of God's goodness. A
word that appears often in the Psalms is *yadah* – meaning to lift hands in
praise. Another is *tehillah* – meaning to break out in unrehearsed song.
The much-used Hebrew word *towdah* is to offer praise and thanksgiving
(often in song) for God's Word being true in the past and the future.
As you make a joyful noise unto the Lord, *zamar* means to worship
with instruments and celebrate in song and music, while *barak* means
to kneel to bless God and adore Him. Worship is much more than
singing a few slow-rhythm songs, and you do not have to be in church
to worship Almightly God.

A primary Hebrew word for worship – *shachah* – means to shout uninhibited praises of adoration in a loud voice to a king or God. It also means to pay obeisance (such as bowing down or being prostrate to show respect). Indeed, even in my culture, bowing down, especially to a king, is an act of worship. In some other cultures, bowing before elderly people is an act of respect or admiration. Bowing to someone is motivated by respect for the individual. It is a way of acknowledging the person's value. Bowing before the king may be accompanied with singing the praises of that king.

Paying obeisance suggests not only external honour but also an internal feeling of respect attached to the external figure. In a way, it doesn't really matter whether you enjoy worship. Your worship is not about you; it is about God Almighty. Although I am certainly not defending poor singing, when it comes to worship, we must focus more on the One we are giving honour to and less on ourselves.

In true worship, the emphasis should be on giving the most excellent praise we can to God. Worship is an act we give to God; it is not something we do just to feel good about ourselves or to make us think that we have completed our part in a church service. Worship is about articulating the awesome glory of God. To worship God is to attribute to Him the highest worth.

According to Jesus, true worship must be done in a specific pattern: "In spirit and in truth." We are created distinct from animals in that we have a spirit. Animals have bodies and souls, but no spirit. We have a spirit, and before we can truly worship God, we must understand who we are. We are created in the image of God. God, who is the Trinity (the Father, the Son, and the Holy Spirit), made us in His image. That means we are triune beings as well. We each have a soul, body, and spirit.

Proverbs 20:27 (AMP) reveals that we receive illumination from the Lord through our spirit. "The spirit of man [that factor in human personality which proceeds immediately from God] is the lamp of the

Lord, searching all his innermost parts." If our spirit is regenerated, we can connect with God in worship. To be a true worshipper, you must know the worth of the Person you are worshipping. The first step to knowing Him is to believe that there is a King who reigns over all. This same King extends love towards us through His Son, Jesus Christ. You can have access to Him only through His Son!

You need to acknowledge that sin entered the human race when Adam disobeyed God in the Garden of Eden and was passed down to all of his and Eve's children. Man lost a unique relationship with the King (God), but His Son, Jesus, came and reconciled us back to the Father. The moment you confess that Jesus Christ is Lord and ask for forgiveness of your sins, you become a new person. The Holy Spirit rejuvenates your spirit. Thus, worship is the *new you* being constantly influenced by the Holy Spirit in a spiritual union of praise. Worship is a call from the King to come before Him and meet with Him in amazement, pleasure, and joy.

You will draw water with joy from the springs of salvation.

Isaiah 12:3

Worshipping God requires you to be joyful. It is a call to know Him intimately and to express gratitude in gladness. Worship is the desire to know the Lord better and being grateful for who He is and what He has done. We need to worship on a regular basis. In fact, I highly recommend taking the time to worship God several times a day. You can worship Him while walking to catch your bus or tram. You can thank Him before and after studying, before and after eating, when you wake up and when you go to bed. You can never thank Him too much. Learn to say, "Thank you, Jesus," all the time. This expressed gratefulness connects you with Him throughout the day.

Adequate worship must be grounded in God's Word. When Jesus prayed to the Father on the night of His betrayal, He said, "Make them holy in the truth; your word is truth" (John 17:17 CEB). For your worship of God to be in truth, it must be in agreement with the Word of God. This is why I love to proclaim who God is according to how the Word of God describes Him. The Psalms have a lot to say about God's person, His attributes, and His wondrous acts. Try worshiping God by reading some of the Psalms, and you will always have praises to offer to Him.

Genesis 2:8 tells us that God originally walked with man. Adam had direct communication with God. In worship, you can enjoy such a relationship with God. God's presence comes down to surround you. You can bring His presence into any and every situation of your life. Worship is the strength of your relationship with God; the more you worship, the stronger you become. Do not restrict your worship to church services. You can worship God anywhere. It is best to give thanks in all situations. You are acknowledging either that God has taken care of your problems or that He will take care of them.

If you refuse to worship God and to give thanks for what He has done in your life, your heart will begin to worship other things.

And instead of worshiping the glorious, ever-living God,
they worshiped idols made to look like mere people,
or birds and animals and snakes.

Romans 1:23

When you remove God from any situation (a relationship, academics, your social life, and so on), someone or something else will take that place of admiration in your life.

I met a man who chose a belief system that would ease his guilt-ridden conscience; he claimed to worship himself. His highest morality was himself. He gave thanks to himself and prayed to himself for forgiveness when he thought he had sinned. This is an example of what may happen when you do not worship the true God. If you do not put God in His rightful place, the spiritual needs of your being must place something else in that position. Failing to be thankful and to glorify God will not only usher in idolatry but will throw open the door for other wicked things to come in. Who are you worshipping today?

THE HIGHEST FORM OF WORSHIP

We need to recognise that Christian worship is more than music. I love the musical aspect of worship because it affects our emotions, and the lyrics can make an impression on our hearts, which can cause us to become lost in the experience. Christian music is a great tool for helping us feel closer to God. It is not uncommon for people to pick a church based solely on the style of its music (worship). Worship, however, is about the position of our hearts, not merely the music. Our hearts must be right with Him. That is why Jesus said we should not worship in the flesh but in the spirit. Our spirit must connect with God (who is Spirit). The highest form of worship is to make worship a way of life. God delights in us when we offer our body, soul, and spirit to Him in worship. For this reason, He takes pleasure when young people keep their bodies pure in honour of Him.

> *I appeal to you therefore, brethren (put your name),*
> *and beg of you in view of [all] the mercies of God, to make a*
> *decisive dedication of your bodies [presenting all your members and*
> *faculties] as a living sacrifice, holy (devoted, consecrated) and well*
> *pleasing to God, which is your reasonable (rational, intelligent)*
> *service and spiritual worship.*

Romans 12:1 (AMP)

Worship is important to God. He created us with an inner need to worship and to connect with something much deeper than our being. Only God is worthy of worship. Worship gladdens God's heart, especially when we go beyond music and lyrics and offer our bodies to Him. When we do that, God is not only pleased, but He infuses strength into us to stay in His presence and fellowship with Him. That is what He desires.

Warmly Yours

Notes

Purity Vow

I (insert name) offer my body unto God as a living sacrifice. My body shall always be holy and acceptable unto God, my Maker. I shall not defile my body, which is the temple of the Lord, through my words and actions. I will live to honour God's commands in all that I think and do. I make this promise in the presence of the Almighty God and by His grace, I shall fulfil my vows. Amen.

CHAPTER 15

JUST DO IT!

Dear Friend,

On my tenth wedding anniversary, I decided to buy a new dress. Surprisingly, this became a stressful decision. I had such a wide range of options to choose from, and I wanted to make the best choice I could. In fact, my options were limited only by budgetary constraints. Life is always like that. We are offered countless choices every day and must make decisions.

Although in many cases our choices do not seem to be monumental and do not shift our lives in significant ways, each choice matters. Some things in life, however, are not viable options if we want a desired outcome. For instance, if we want to live healthy lives, it is not an option to eat junk food all day every day. Similarly, not paying taxes is also not a viable option in the UK if we want to avoid facing potentially serious consequences. Likewise, we should not treat certain things as optional in our Christian life. Obeying the Lord is not an option. It should be something we do all the time. Obedience is yielding to what God says in His Word, which comes to us either through personal reading or through any vessel God uses (priests, parents, teachers, friends, or anyone in a position of authority).

RELATING TO GOD THROUGH HIS WORD

Although I was not an avid reader as a teenager, I realized that reading the Bible was inevitable if I wanted to have a solid relationship with God. I found the interesting Bible stories fascinating, of course, but I was encouraged to study the Scriptures. This required me to take notes and write down questions about confusing topics. Fortunately, I made a conscious effort to associate with godly older friends (seniors) who influenced and encouraged me not only to study God's Word but to meditate (think deeply on) and apply it. Meditation is the crucial part of relating to the Word of God. That is how you will find treasures in this holy book.

When I was thirteen or fourteen years old, I had a close male friend. I never considered him a boyfriend because he didn't ask me out at that time and we never kissed or went out to fun places together. We did like being around each other. We attended different boarding schools, and whenever we were on holiday, it was difficult not being able to talk to or see him. One day after my personal prayers, I began flipping through my old King James Version of the Bible hoping that God would give me a specific instruction about my relationship with this guy.

Soon after, I picked a Bible passage from Proverbs to study. Suddenly, like a vision, I knew that I should read Proverbs 9:12. To my amazement, it was a specific instruction! "If thou be wise, thou shalt be wise for thyself: but if thou scornest, thou alone shalt bear it." It was so frightening, and I could not believe that I could actually hear God. I was pleasantly surprised, too.

I began to meditate on this verse of the Bible that I had never heard or read in my life. It was never preached to me in church, but God was speaking to me, telling me that if I continued in this relationship, there would be grave consequences. Know that this instruction came only because I was meditating on the Scriptures and not just casually flipping through the Bible. Although I tried to dissociate myself from this young man, he applied a lot of pressure on me to keep the relationship going, and I often reconsidered the situation. But you know what? God knew why He did not want me to stay in the relationship with this young man. He was the guy I mentioned in Chapter 11 who later tried to rape me when I went to pick up a cassette tape from his brother that my sister wished to borrow.

I recently reviewed certain areas of my life. In considering my marriage, I thought "it has been a pleasant journey so far." I then probed further and asked, "What are the things that have worked for me?" It came to me that our success was partly because I had learned to be obedient in certain things. When older and godly women told me to do something, I just did it! Sometimes I didn't understand, and sometimes I received advice from those who were not following their own advice, but if it came from the Lord or His Word, I just did it. The Bible warns us not to be a hearer of the Word only but to be a doer of the Word. What good is the Word if you recite it, sing it, or even preach it but do not do it?

Nowadays, especially in the more developed countries, we tend to view a lot of things as optional. We even treat God that way. He is just an option. We convince ourselves that as long as we are not doing something really bad, He will simply forgive us if we live our lives our own way and for our own benefit.

Living for ourselves means that we do not have to place importance on God's Word, and we do not have fear the Lord (King James Version's way of saying respect and revere Him). Proverbs 1:7 and 9:10 tell us that fear of the Lord is the beginning of wisdom. If we do not respect and revere God and know His power, we are just plain stupid (the opposite of wisdom). If you read the book of Proverbs, you learn that you need to value the Word of God by doing as it says. You need to get wisdom at all costs. Wisdom is knowing the right thing to do and making a decision to do it. When you obey, you become wise. The Word of God should not just be a good book to us. It should be the guiding principle for our daily lives.

Understanding is what prompts us to obey. Psalm 119:32 (CEV) says, "I am eager to learn all that you want me to do; help me to understand more and more." When you understand the Word of God, you are enlightened and your heart is glad. You will be motivated to obey His commands. Obedience becomes easier when we understand that His commands are mainly for our benefit.

Tips for Studying the Word of God

1. Set a regular time.
2. Prepare: Choose a place, get a pen, some paper, and your chosen Bible version.
3. Invite God: Pray for understanding. You can access deep secrets in the Word.
4. Shut out distractions: Turn off your phone, tablet, etc.
5. Be open and teachable: God's Word judges our innermost thoughts.
6. Ask questions and take notes.
7. Consider using a daily devotional.

Obeying God and His Word is vital and beneficial; not obeying God and His Word is very costly – even deadly in some cases. Remember Samson. When he disobeyed, the strength of the Almighty left him. His strength fled him not simply because his hair had been cut but because he had grieved the Spirit of God through his disobedience. When Samson again trusted in the LORD, however, his hair grew back, and his strength came back. What a loving God we serve!

Our God is not the God of a second chance, but of another chance, and another chance, and another … I encourage you to make up your mind to be a doer who actively responds to God's Word.

I made a conscious decision that whenever I heard something from God's Word, I would not question it because God rewards obedience. It is time we just did it!

Are you struggling in any area of your life? God is beautiful for every situation. He can fix it for you if you ask Him. He loves you so much, and His loving arms are open wide to receive *you*. One thing is sure: If you desire to have a close relationship with God, He will grant you the grace. He will receive you once He sees your desire. Most importantly, you will need to respond to Him in obedience. Obedience guarantees that you will develop and sustain a deeper relationship with God. His strength is appropriated only through obedience. Dare to respond to God's Word in obedience.

Dear Friend, always remember that He (God) who has started a good work in you will complete it. I am convinced that you will excel in all things through God. Most importantly, let us forget about the things behind us (past mistakes, hurts, struggles, disappointments, and even our trophies) and reach out for the things ahead of us. Keep on pressing towards the goal – the prize of the upward call of God in Christ Jesus (Philippians 3:14).

Warmly Yours

CHAPTER 16

FOR YOUR EYES ONLY

Dear Friend,

There are some words that I have been pondering over for a while. You must have read this in the Bible or heard it said: "Give not that which is holy to the dogs, neither cast your pearls before swine, lest they trample them under their feet, and turn again and rend you." I thought long and hard about this Bible verse. Why did Jesus use the word *pearls*, and why would a seeming act of kindness—giving a precious stone to the swine— attract such a horrible payback? After extensive research, I discovered that pearls had certain noteworthy qualities that explain our authenticity as girls or ladies. I think I should also inform you that whenever a precious gem is given to someone who is mindless and careless like a hog, such a person will be drained and left with nothing valuable.

Jesus tells us that we are not to give what is holy to dogs (Matthew 7:6). What is holy is anything that is set apart, chaste, undefiled, and Christ-like rather than worldly. In other words, God sees those who are saved as holy, and we should not give away this precious gift of holiness that cost God His only Son. Many people will try to influence us, deceive us, give us false information, and just hoodwink us into believing that the precious gift of chastity is not a big deal. Please do not believe this lie! We are not to disrespect ourselves—we who are the very vessels of the Holy Spirit—by letting others abuse us or lead us astray. The truth is that we should love those in the world, but we should not conduct ourselves as they do nor be overpowered by their principles and values.

We should take Jesus' warning very seriously. Undoubtedly, we must be prone to such carelessness, or the Bible would not have to instruct us against it. *Do not throw your pearls before swine.* Swine eat leftovers—slop, not precious stones, and they are content with doing so because that is what they are. Have you been to a farm and seen pigs? They are filthy animals that enjoy rolling in mud and in their own waste. So why would a person give a shiny, valuable gem to such an animal? Dear Precious Pearl, we may sometimes get carried away by our emotions and our desire to be loved and accepted by others thereby engaging in intimate relationships. Be aware that nobody loves and accepts us like Jesus does.

PEARLS ARE COSTLY

Egyptian royals were often buried with pearls. Medieval princesses were often decorated with delicate pearl necklaces, and medieval knights also wore pearls. Pearls are valuable and precious. Until the early 1900s, natural pearls were accessible only to the wealthy and famous. Little wonder then that the Bible compared us to pearls. It shows that a precious girl like you should not be found engaging in immorality or any form of sexual looseness. Your lifestyle should be to detest and flee from impurity in thoughts, words, and deeds.

Sexual sin is one form of sin that we should avoid like a plague. Any other sin that a man commits is one outside the body, but he who commits sexual immorality sins against his own body.

Do you not know that your body is the temple (the very sanctuary)
of the Holy Spirit who lives within you, whom you have received
[as a Gift] from God? You are not your own, you were bought with

*a price (purchased with a preciousness and paid for, made His
own). So then, honour God and bring glory to Him in your body.*

1 Corinthians 6:20 (AMP).

God is definitely interested in your body because that is where His
Spirit seeks to dwell. God is also interested in your mind, which is your
soul and your spirit, the source of power and control for both your body
and soul. He wants you whole in all areas. When you engage in premarital
sex, you are not only sinning against God, but against yourself.

Dear Friend, can I remind you again that you are very expensive? You
are precious and unique! You are classy, and you need to treat yourself in
that manner and not allow anyone to treat you as anything less. You need
to know who you are. You are the valued daughter of the Most High! (1
Peter 2:9). Do not misuse or abuse your body. Generally speaking, we
refer to abuse as ill-treatment, hurt, or harm to a person. It is the misuse
or mishandling of someone or something. You are created for a purpose,
and you are the idea of the only wise God. He clearly specifies how you
should use your body and mind. If you act contrary to His instructions,
then you are abusing yourself.

When social workers conduct assessments of needs in cases of
abuse, they do not look only at the child's physical appearance.
They need information on different areas of development such as
health, environmental factors, education, emotional and behavioural
development, identity, and so on to complete a robust assessment. In
the same way, God is not interested only in your body but also in your
mind and soul. He wants everything about you to be whole and intact. It
is totally unsafe to use your entire being in a way that is not commanded
and designed by God. Your being is created to honour and worship God.
It is not for sexual immorality, wickedness, or abusing drugs and alcohol.
If you truly believe that you are costly, bought with a price, you will not
fall cheaply for any of these vices. Remember, you are a precious gem!

PEARLS ARE RARE

The origin of a pearl is truly a miraculous incident. Pearls are uncommon, exceptional, and special. Pearls are not found on the surface or just down the street. A pearl is truly a treasure. That is who you are! So you should not be found in every night party or loitering around on the street with people who have no appreciation of your true value. This is not to say that you shouldn't have friends and have fun, but remember that birds of a feather flock together. Keep your distance from those whose actions and words can pollute your mind. Guard your heart uncompromisingly!

PEARLS ARE AUTHENTIC

To be authentic is to be genuine, unfailing, dependable, and real. God wants us to grow to maturity and be dependable. Pearls are not counterfeit; they are genuine. Dear Friend, dare to be yourself! Do not imitate others or seek approval of the crowd. Do not be less than what the Word of God declares you to be! I encourage you to have a sound, whole way of life and not to live a double life. Open your heart to God and let your *yes* be *yes* and your *no* be *no*.

PEARLS ARE BEAUTIFUL

In contrast to gemstones or precious metals that must be mined from the earth, pearls are developed by live oysters far below the surface of the sea. Gemstones must be cut and refined to bring forth or reveal their beauty, but pearls need no such treatment to make known their loveliness. They are born from oysters complete with a sparkling iridescence, with a gleaming and soft inner glow unlike any other gem in the world. You are simply unrivaled in your beauty—inner and outer beauty. You don't need anyone to convince you that you are a total beauty! So why do you need the media or a pop idol to define how you should look? You don't need cosmetic surgery to correct your nose or any other part of your body. You are not an accident, and there is no mistake about you at all. You don't have to look malnourished to be gorgeous; you are already beautiful. Therefore, honour God with your beauty and flee from all appearances of evil that could tarnish your beauty.

And God saw everything that he had made,
and behold, it was very good.

Genesis 1:31

Oh yes, you shaped me first inside, then out; you formed me in my
mother's womb. I thank you, High God—you're breathtaking!
Body and soul, I am marvellously made!

Psalm 139:14

PEARLS ARE DEDICATED
TO THE NOBLE

Nobility refers to the idea of belonging to or constituting a hereditary class that has special social or political status in a country or state. Since pearls were so highly valued, some European countries passed laws forbidding anyone but the nobles to wear them. You are *God's Pearl of Great Price*! You have been dedicated to the only righteous and blameless God.

Dear Friend, I encourage you today to set yourself apart and detach from anything that could lead you to give your precious pearls to undeserving pigs. These pearls will be your crowning glory, your beauty and evidence that you believe that you have a purpose to fulfil on Earth. There are things that you cannot be involved in because you have a definite assignment and mission to accomplish. Certainly, there are things that you must refuse to do, even things that the world celebrates. You must make a firm decision and be resolved not to change your mind. The Holy Spirit is ever present to support and empower you in your decision to live a blameless life.

Finally, these six reasons can help you make a wise decision to worship God with your mind and body:

1. The devil doesn't love you and will seek to destroy you. Develop inner strength and resist his suggestions!
2. The 'world' will lie to you about the purpose of sex. Only believe in the Word of God; it is ever true.
3. Your body does not belong to you. It belongs to God, therefore; glorify Him in your body by abstaining from sexual immorality. Thinking about having sex? Think about long term, not short term.
4. God is kind. He will not give you instruction that is impossible for you to obey. God's command is not burdensome or harsh.
5. God wants the best for you. Never forget that He has your best interest in mind!
6. Lastly, there is a reward! God has a record; He will not forget to give you your prize. Galatians 6:9

Dear Friend, I commit you to the grace of God that can teach and guide you to live a discreet and upright life. May you experience and enjoy the grace of God that brings salvation to mankind. Keep loving the Lord. I love you!

Warmly Yours

REFERENCES

A Brief History of Pearls. (n.d.). Retrieved July 20, 2016, from http://www.americanpearl.com/ahistory.html

Common English Bible. (2011). Nashville: Common English Bible.

Kay, K. (1995, February 11). What the Bible says about Worship. Retrieved May 4, 2016, from http://www.bible.ca/ef/topical-what-the-bible-says-about-worship.htm

Laurie, G. (n.d.). Devotions and Blogs - Harvest: Greg Laurie. Retrieved May 4, 2016, from https://www.harvest.org/devotions-and-blogs

Pratte, D. E. (n.d.). The Gospel Way Bible Study Guide. Retrieved May 4, 2016, from http://www.gospelway.com/

The Holy Bible: Amplified Bible (1987). La Habra, CA: The Lockman Foundation.

The message: The Bible in contemporary language. (2002). Colorado Springs: NavPress.

What does God say about masturbation in scripture? (n.d.). Retrieved May 4, 2016, from http://www.whataboutjesus.com/

Wilkins, M. and Kristopherson, K. (1980). One day at at time [Recorded by Cristy Lane]. On One day at at time [Album]. Hollywood, CA: United Artists Records.

You can contact/interact with
me via email at

**oliveadebola@gmail.com
and on Facebook.**

Note from the Publisher

Are you a first time author?

Not sure how to proceed to get your book published?
Want to keep all your rights and all your royalties?
Want it to look as good as a Top 10 publisher?
Need help with editing, layout, cover design?
Want it out there selling in 90 days or less?

Visit our website for some exciting new options!

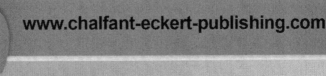

www.chalfant-eckert-publishing.com

Made in the USA
Charleston, SC
11 October 2016